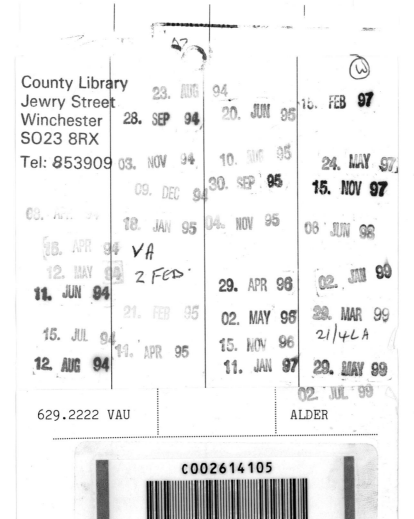

VAUXHALL
THE POSTWAR YEARS

TREVOR ALDER

Foulis

Haynes

®

A **Foulis** Motoring Book

First published 1991

Published by:
Haynes Publishing Group
Sparkford, Nr Yeovil
Somerset BA22 7JJ, England

Haynes Publications Inc
861 Lawrence Drive, Newbury Park,
California 91320, USA

**British Library Cataloguing in
Publication Data**

    The history of Vauxhall cars.
    1. Cars
    1. Title
    629.2222

    ISBN 0 85429 746 4

Library of Congress Catalog Card Number
90–84479

Editor: Robin Read
Design and Layout: Jill Moulton
Typeset in Plantin Roman 11/12pt and
printed in England by J.H. Haynes & Co. Ltd.

Contents

Introduction

Vauxhall's products are more popular now than ever before. With a seemingly ever increasing sales percentage of the British market, it is now high time for a complete history covering the postwar years and detailing the cars and light commercials of this successful company.

A large spectrum of models has evolved since the Second World War, the starting point for this publication. From the humble but successful Ten to modern four-wheel-drive Cavaliers, any factory-built Vauxhall, and indeed many outside conversions, are covered in this book.

I have had great pleasure in producing this Vauxhall history, which through its text and its photographs is intended to give the reader, for the first time in such detail, a comprehensive account of the subject. As would be expected, it has not been easy. Some of the information has been lost in the mists of time; other already tinted facts can get highly coloured by enthusiastic owners. Perhaps most important of all, I have tried to keep to photographs that are either of the period, or of concours vehicles in standard form, and to stay away from the "show shots" sadly so often seen in other specialist marque publications.

Included in each chapter there is a complete table of *all* models produced in the categories described. It will be seen that in more recent years each specific model has more variants under its name. It would have been easy for some limited editions (of which there are so many now!) to be forgotten or overlooked. Hopefully this has not happened, as I have been up more avenues of research than I care to remember. Naturally, details of the current models in production can only be complete and correct up to the point when this book went to press in 1990.

In the late Eighties, the name Opel had disappeared from Vauxhall's sales brochures, after the departure of the exclusive Monza and Manta models. West Germany's Opel cars had featured alongside Vauxhall's products since 1981; because of their short joint run, however, I have tried to refrain from describing Opel models, concentrating on Vauxhall only.

Vauxhall once manufactured solely at the Luton plant. In 1963, production was extended to the newly completed all modern Ellesmere Port factory on the south side of the River Mersey. Dunstable's manufacturing plant was confined to commercials only. Some vehicles are now also manufactured in Spain and Germany, and share many common parts with other cars manufactured by the giant General Motors company.

Long may they continue!

Trevor Alder

Acknowledgements

No one can write a comprehensive book of this nature without help from other sources. I am indebted to so many individuals who so helpfully gave up their spare time — many hours at a stretch in some cases.

The strength of this book I believe, lies in the numerous photographs that are contemporary with the cars depicted; these mainly came from deep in the recesses of the Vauxhall press office in Luton. The person here who really must be thanked is Miriam Carroll without whose help, I feel sure, this book would have been less interesting. Miriam allowed me much time researching and digging around in various files, until I came up with the varied selection of photographic material offered in the book. A big thank you to you, Miriam. Help also came from other sources at Luton, particularly the Vauxhall service department.

The identical twins Mario and Edmund Lindsay were untiring in their efforts to help me gather and compile some of the information presented in this project. Their hospitality was tremendous; it is no understatement to say that these two gentlemen must surely go down in history as Vauxhall's number one enthusiasts. Their combined archive sections are some of the most comprehensive and most splendidly laid-out libraries I have ever seen devoted to one make, and must certainly be the best outside a museum. Their enthusiasm stretches to owning two unique prototypes — both important milestones in Vauxhall's history during the 1970s — and both featured in this book.

Of course, organizations are also always valuable in this kind of work, and I made much use of the library in the National Motor Museum at Beaulieu. Some of the earliest pictures in this book were loaned to me by this museum.

Anybody with more than a remote interest in motor history or renovation will have visited, or at least have heard of, the modest bookshop Chaters in Isleworth, West London. Much of the groundwork material was bought there after many hours delving in the second-hand book sections and magazine basement.

My great friend Lindon Lait patiently assisted me throughout with visits to all the above places, and it is to him that I am indebted for the very idea of writing a book on the marque in the first instance! Thank you for your time, Lindon.

Much of the research would certainly not have been possible without the assistance of the two great motoring weeklies, namely *Autocar* and *Motor*. Long may the amalgamated *Autocar & Motor* magazine continue. I am also grateful to these two motoring weeklies for permission to reproduce the majority of the so easily forgotten splendid cutaway drawings from years gone by of the then new models, which have added a considerable element of interest.

Thanks also to my learned friend Martin Cooper, who on his two-year global tour, has sent me many reports of Vauxhalls abroad and many photographs and to Paula, my wife, for all her help.

Finally, sincere thanks must go to all those owners concerned with the photography specially undertaken — there are too many names to mention here. Thank you for your time, and more importantly for the fact that you all keep your vehicles in such good order and still on the road!

Trevor Alder
Ipswich

1

The Early Postwar Years

During the First World War the Vauxhall factory at Luton in Bedfordshire was an important producer of 25 hp staff cars for the Government. It was a rather different story in the Second World War when the authorities had other plans for the plant: between 1939 and 1945 its skilled workforce was to produce 250,000 Bedford trucks and over 5500 Churchill tanks and undertook important wartime development work, including the manufacture of anything from ammunition to lifeboats. So it was that all car production came to a total halt in 1939 for six years, except for a hundred or so cars built for the armed services.

Vehicles affected by the ceasing of production in 1939 included the new Vauxhall Ten Type H, in both four-door saloon and now rare two-door coupé forms; its big brother the 12 hp I type; and the larger six-cylinder 14 hp J. The six-cylinder 25 hp GY and GL models (remarkably cheap at £298) of 1936 had already been discontinued. As an example of the magnitude of production in a complete year, 59,968 cars and trucks were produced in 1938.

Of course, after the war it took a considerable time to reorganize the factory for civilian production. This, coupled with the fact that raw materials were now in very short supply, meant that it was not until well into 1946 that new private cars were once again leaving the Luton factory in any significant numbers.

Basically, the same line-up was offered as before the war; the Ten (although unfortunately, the attractive Ten coupé had gone), Twelve and Fourteen models. The Government called for an export drive, and so most of these were for the continental market. Evidence exists in the Vauxhall archives of 53,586 vehicles being produced in 1946 alone. In September 1947 came the disappearance of the popular little Ten, as new taxation rules meant there was little point in continuing with the smaller-engined vehicles. In total 55,000 Tens were produced, and a small model would not be sold again until the arrival of the HA Viva in the early 1960s. The excuse was that building just two models would simplify production, and the *Vauxhall Motorist* of 1947 was quick to point out that existing orders for the Ten would be filled by 12 hp cars. In reality, it was less than a year later that the L types started to roll off the production line ready for the 1948 London Motor Show.

There was quite a noticeable styling gap between the cars of the 1950s and the immediate postwar products. This was partly due to the fact that in America peace time manufacture and design changes had continued into the early 1940s: Britain had to catch up! These new L types of 1948 bridged that gap, having rather upright, older-looking passenger compartments, yet modern boots, flat radiator grilles and column gearchanges. There were two L types, rather similar in outward appearance, but quite different underneath. The 1.5-litre Wyvern was a four-cylinder and won much praise for its 35 mpg economy — the reader should be reminded that these were the days of petrol rationing. The *Autocar* magazine stated: "Every gallon of petrol gives very good value". There is a public house in Luton called The Wyvern, an establishment that was apparently named not after the mythical beast, but after the car!

Although its production did not continue after the Second World War, the 1203 cc ohv Vauxhall Ten coupé H type was part of the Ten range that ran until autumn 1947. At £198 about 15 per cent more expensive than the standard Ten, the two door coupé was styled by David Jones. He was Vauxhall's head of styling in the 1950s, 1960s and early 1970s, and was also responsible for the Firenza coupé based on the Viva HC bodyshell peer carefully and you can see a similarity! The bodywork was by Pressed Steel.

Model	Ten (H)
Dates of Production	October 1937 to 1939; early 1946 to September 1947
Body Types	4-door saloon, 2-door coupé (pre-war only)
Engines Offered	1203 cc, 4-cylinder
Transmission	3-speed manual
Average Fuel Consumption	over 40 mpg
Top Speed	over 60 mph
Braking System	Lockheed hydraulic, (drums)
Dimensions	Length: 13 ft 2 $\frac{1}{2}$ in; width: 5ft 1in
Weight	18 cwt
Production Changes	1940 season: longer and wider bodies
Price at Launch	£168 (saloon)
Made at	Luton
Number Produced	42,245 (pre-war); approx. 13,000 (post-war)

The other L type was a straight-six (Vauxhall had been building these for many years and even today, when the closest competition insists on V engines, the firm still produces straight-six units to power its Senators and Carltons). This second L type was named the Velox: the name itself was far from new, for in 1913 it was used for the 30/98. The Velox was a powerful car, with its flat six unit capable of winding up to 75 mph on the flat, which was quite respectable for the time. These stylish new models were subject to a special dealers' introduction on 24 August 1948 at Luton. Here 150 new Veloxes were driven away by these eager dealers after the day's proceedings bound for towns and cities all over Britain. Each car bore a proud "For a Home Motorist" label. The 10-day 1948 London Motor Show, the first such British event for 10 years, hosted the official launch of the new models. A year later Vauxhall launched these new L types in a similar fashion down-under. The Vauxhall "Drive-away" took place in Melbourne, Australia, when a gleaming line of the new models left the S.A. Cheney showrooms in Flinders Street.

Production continued, with only minor modifications announced at the London Motor Show in 1949: the Velox was to have larger tyres, and all models now had bigger headlamps, a new steering box, and most strikingly a new range of Metallichrome colours. The more basic Wyvern now had leather seats as standard. These L types ran from their introduction in 1948 until 1951, and in that period they were the only Vauxhalls in production, alongside the sister Bedford trucks. Although rarer in these earlier days, conversions did exist. Two interesting such conversions were the 400 kg (880 lb) payload L type Velox by Geser of Lucerne, made albeit in rather limited numbers for the Swiss Post Office; while the Holden Calèche sports tourer with drophead was popular in Australia.

In all, over 130,000 L types were manufactured in a three-year production run, the larger proportion under the Velox badge.

The new Ten of 1937 proved to be of great engineering interest it was the first Vauxhall to have unitary construction of the body and chassis, although Opel had been using this method of manufacture since 1935. Despite its high performance for the day, its key points were its very low running cost (up to 40 mpg) and low purchase price. Vauxhall made a strong selling point with the economy aspect — and the Ten sold very quickly indeed. So much so that the Luton plant was expanded, and the workforce there enlarged. Ten thousand of the new little Tens were bought within five months; the revolutionary Ten was thus an instant success. Very few Tens survive. The British climate has unfortunately meant that most have met their end through corrosion.

The Fourteen (Series J) was in production from October 1938 until war was declared in September 1939, and production picked up again after the conflict until its departure in 1948. Essentially it was a large car, bigger than the Twelve, with a 1781 cc six-cylinder engine of some 14 hp. It differed in every aspect from its 1930s forerunner except in bore, stroke and hp rating. Although semi-elliptic leaf springs were still used at the rear, a new anti-roll device allowed uncannily good roadholding. Despite a large wheelbase and track, the 1939 season Fourteen was actually lighter than its forerunner.

Model	Twelve (I)
Dates of Production	1939–40; 1946 to August 1948
Body Types	4-door saloon
Engines Offered	1442 cc, 4-cylinder
Transmission	3-speed manual
Average Fuel Consumption	35 mpg
Top Speed	over 65 mph
Braking System	Hydraulic, (drums)
Dimensions	Length: 13 ft 2½ in; width: 5ft 1in
Weight	18 cwt
Production Changes	Pre-war body continued until March 1946; divided grilles from 1940
Price at Launch	£198
Made at	Luton
Number Produced	10,164 (including pre-war cars)

Vauxhall's entry in the 1939 RAC Rally Ten (left), Twelve (centre) and J Type Fourteen.
No road section prizes were awarded to the Barnes brothers' Autosports team, but the Ten (this
one had already run in the Monte Carlo Rally) did gain a first in the coachwork competition
for closed cars under £200. Quite clear here is the similar appearance of the three models —
right down to the chrome-plated bonnet flutes.

Model	Fourteen (J)
Dates of Production	1939–40; 1946 to August 1948
Body Types	4-door saloon
Engines Offered	1781 cc, 6-cylinder
Transmission	3-speed manual, full synchromesh
Average Fuel Consumption	22 mpg
Top Speed	70 mph
Braking System	Hydraulic (drums)
Dimensions	Length: 14 ft; width: 5ft 3in
Weight	$2\frac{1}{2}$ cwt
Wheels and Tyres	Tyres 5.50 x 16
Production Changes	No chrome radiator grille surround not fitted after the war
Price at Launch	£235
Made at	Luton
Number Produced	45,499 (including pre-war cars)

Vauxhall J Fourteen (left) and I Twelve. Immediate postwar production included both these models, and of course the Ten. After the war the Twelve was produced at first with the 1940-style six-light body (although without the chrome radiator sur-round), but from March 1946 it shared its body with the Ten, as shown here. It used a 1442 cc 35 bhp four-cylinder engine and longer wheelbase.

The L types were the first new postwar Vauxhalls. The Velox and Wyverns arrived in August 1948, and were the only models produced by the company until superseded in 1951 by the E types. The L types bridged the styling gap between the now elderly-looking pre-war H, I and J types, and the later Es. The Velox had a 2.25-litre straight-six engine (with 75 mph top speed). The Wyvern won much praise for its economy with its 1.5-litre straight-four; up to 35 mpg was easily attainable. The L types were the first Vauxhalls to feature column gear changes.

Model	Wyvern & Velox L Types
Dates of Production	August 1948–July 1951
Body Types	4-door saloon
Engines Offered	1442 cc, 4-cylinder (Wyvern)
	2275 cc, 6-cylinder (Velox)
Transmission	3-speed manual
Average Fuel Consumption	30 mpg (Wyvern)
	22 mpg (Velox)
Top Speed	60 mph (Wyvern)
	74 mph (Velox)
0-50 Mph	27.8 sec (Wyvern)
	19.3 sec (Velox)
Braking System	Lockheed hydraulic, (drums)
Wheels and Tyres	Steel wheels; tyres: 5.00 x 16 (Wyvern);
	5.25 x 16 (Velox)
Dimensions	Length: 13 ft 8½ in; width: 5 ft 2 in
Weight	2184 lb (Wyvern)
	2464 lb (Velox)
Production Changes	September 1949: introduction of Metal-lichrome paint; new steering gear; larger headlamps and separate parking lamps set in the wings
Price at Launch	£550 3s 11d (Velox)
	£479 (Wyvern)
Made at	Luton
Number Produced	55,409 (Wyvern)
	76,919 (Velox)

This photograph was originally taken for the National Schools of Motoring Journal no doubt with a suitable caption suggesting how easy the car would have been for a learner driver. This L type six-cylinder Velox (identified as a Velox rather than a Wyvern by its front overriders and cream-coloured wheels) was basically an H type with new front and rear end treatment. The name Velox was not new it had first been used for the sporty 30/98 model in pre-war years. Vauxhall had, at last, moved away from its previously upright radiator style to the kind depicted here, and the bold move was taken to house the headlamp units within the mudguards. The L type lasted until the 1951 Motor Show, when superseded by an even more modern E type.

Another L type Velox, of 1948 this time and without front side lamp units. The L type brought a rear-hinged bonnet until that time vehicles had had their bonnets split, and hinged in the middle. Pressmen were soon to point out that, "the makers have made no provision for a starting handle". Clearer here are the cream-coloured wheels the cellulosed wheels of the 1.5-litre four-cylinder Wyvern L type shared the bodywork colour. New Metallichrome colours were offered in blue, grey, green and fawn (Velox only). Prices Wyvern £450; Velox £480.

Model	Engine	From	To
IMMEDIATE POSTWAR PERIOD			
Ten (H)	1203	early 46	9/47
Ten H De Luxe	1203	early 46	9/47
Twelve (I) pre-war body *	1442	early 46	3/46
Twelve (I)	1442	3/46	8/48
Fourteen (J)	1781	early 46	8/48
L TYPES			
Wyvern	1442	10/48	7/51
Velox	2275	10/48	7/51

* Very rare, few produced

2

The Mid-1950s

Almost by default it seemed, Vauxhall was to announce a brand-new model at the London Motor Show every three years, so it did not come as too much of a surprise when a completely new family of Velox and Wyvern models arrived in 1951. These were longer, wider and lower cars than their L type forerunners. Many of the square lines had been rounded off, and the occupants sat much lower. It was no secret that their common design owed much to their 1949 General Motors cousins from Chevrolet. Ford had exhibited their American-influenced new models — the Zephyr Six and Consul — at the previous year's Motor Show. Ford and Vauxhall both offered a four-cylinder engine in a new body and sold in competition for several years.

Once again, the Wyvern was powered by the same 1.5-litre four-cylinder unit, and the Velox models shared the 2.25-litre straight-six. However, it was, oddly enough, as early as April 1952 that the new "square" engines were announced for these cars, which remained at the same price. Again, those distinctive bonnet flutes appeared and, just as on the previous cars, they were chrome-plated.

Prototypes went on trial both in Britain, in Porlock (repeated stop–start tests), and on the Continent, in France (high-speed testing) and Switzerland (engine cooling and performance at high altitudes). A £400,000 paint plant had recently been completed at Luton, and all new Velox and Wyverns now boasted a better overall finish, and — more importantly — a better protection against rust.

Within a week of the introduction of the new models, a Velox (the first on the island) took first place in a *concours d'élégance* in Jersey organized by the Jersey Motorcycle and Light Car Club. The prize was awarded by the *Jersey Evening Post* for the most elegant ensemble of car and lady!

Basically, the Wyvern and Velox were virtually identical from the outside, apart from obvious badge differences and of course, to the keen listener, the exhaust note. The Velox by now had overriders as standard, and even its up-market sister's cream-coloured wheels. This continued for three years until the end of 1954, when considerable design changes were made. The larger tubular-type, rather American chrome front end was discontinued in favour of a simpler grille design, and a wider bonnet was employed.

The new E type Wyvern launched in August 1951 brought a new dimension to motoring in Great Britain. This 1.5-litre four-cylinder Wyvern differed from previous L type models in its more up-to-date styling and side-opening bonnet. Note that the chromium-plated bonnet scoops had been carried through to this design. The model sold for £474 plus £265 7s 9d purchase tax. Styling influences from the advanced American models were already evident here the E type was similar in appearance to the Chevrolet Powerglide of the early 1950s. The six-cylinder Velox had a creditable top speed of 75 mph; the four-cylinder 1.5-litre Wyvern was commended for attaining up to 35 mpg. Both the Velox and Wyvern E types had steering column gearchange.

Model	Wyvern, Velox & Cresta E Types
Dates of Production	August 1951 to early 1957 (Wyvern)
	August 1951 to October 1957 (Velox)
	October 1954 to October 1957 (Cresta)
Body Types	4-door saloon; proprietary estates by outside manufacturers
Engines Offered	1442 cc, 4-cylinder; 2275 cc, 6-cylinder, then 1507 cc, 4-cylinder; 2262 cc, 6-cylinder
Transmission	3-speed manual (varying ratios, 4- and 6-cylinder models)
Average Fuel Consumption	4-cylinder: 35 mpg; 6-cylinder: 24 mpg
Top Speed	4-cylinder: 70 mph; 6-cylinder: 80 mph
0-50 Mph	20.0 sec (Wyvern)
	14.3 sec (Velox)
Braking System	Lockheed hydraulic (drums)
Wheels and Tyres	Perforated steel wheels; tyres: 5.60 x 15 (Wyvern); 5.90 x 15 (Velox)
Dimensions	Length: 14 ft $4\frac{1}{2}$ in; width: 5ft 7 in; height: 5ft $3\frac{1}{2}$ in
Weight	2300 lb (Wyvern)
	2450 lb (Velox)
	2541 lb (Cresta)
Production Changes	New engines from April 1952; extensive facelift, 1954; numerous other changes during production life, i.e. larger windows from October 1955. Cresta introduced October 1954
Price at Launch	£740 7s 9d (Wyvern)
	£802 12s 3d (Velox)
Made at	Luton
Number Produced	110,588 (Wyvern)
	235,296 (Velox/Cresta)

The six-cylinder Velox was joined by an even more up-market stablemate, introduced in 1954. This was the Cresta, a name that would appear in the sales brochure until 1972. The EIPC Cresta, like the Velox, had "modesty covers" over the rear wheels (so often seen on Citroën models in the 1970s) and was often seen in two-tone paintwork (matching the two-tone leather interior) and whitewall tyres. The Cresta sold in direct competition with Ford's new up-market, 1954 Zodiac — and outsold it many times over.

In 1956 there were late — but not the last — design changes before the PA models of 1957 were brought in. E types were built with a larger wrap-around rear screen and thinner windscreen pillars for improved visibility. Final changes came in 1957, when electric windscreen wipers were adopted, and even more side chrome! At last the Wyvern could boast those rear-wheel covers, but within a few months this model had been discontinued. When replaced by the PA series, nearly 342,000 E types had been sold since the model's first appearance.

The E types were the basis of more conversions than ever before. In Australia, for example where Vauxhalls were sold in direct competition with Holden, many of them reached pick-up truck status, while the soft-top Vagabond replaced the L type Calèche. In Britain, as far as the factory was concerned, three official estate conversions were available, the first from the Grosvenor group in London (pictured) with its love it/hate it styling. Later came another from Grosvenor, much more car-based, but equally as appalling to look at and named the Swansong. By far the best of the trio was the Dormobile from Martin Walter, who was responsible for many Vauxhall car conversions up to the late 1960s.

The E types formed the basis of many conversions during the 1950s. An unusual combination of chrome and wood is seen here on a newly converted Grosvenor shooting brake as early as December 1953. Similar in style to many American station wagons (wood panelling along the body flanks was far from new to the Americans, for this idea had been adopted for their equivalents of the estate car or shooting brake some 12 years before), and quickly followed by Morris and others in Britain during the 1950s, this Grosvenor was produced until 1956. It was then replaced by the Grosvenor Swansong (£1126). This was much more car-like an all-steel vehicle, with an unusual horizontally split folding rear tailgate, and polished oak-faced plywood with aluminium channels in the rear load area. A further, slightly cheaper conversion by Martin Walter was the Dormobile — perhaps the best looking of the trio. Martin Walter Ltd, of Folkestone, went on for many years converting light commercial vehicles into motor caravans and, of course, producing Cresta estate conversions into the late 1960s.

Whitewalled cross-plyed tyres were the order of the day in this 1957 E type Cresta, powered by the same 2262 cc six-cylinder engine as the Velox. The Cresta was a late arrival in the E type range; it was launched in 1954 as a super-luxury version of the Velox. Note the two-tone paint treatment bordered by chromium strips.

An airbrush artist's view of the six-cylinder Velox engine of 1953, which replaced the original E type engine within 12 months of the model's announcement.

Inset: One of the last E types built was this 1957 Wyvern. It followed in the footsteps of the 341,625 E types built between 1951 and 1957. The E type — the first Vauxhall to bring in curved windscreens — underwent several changes in its production life, including extra brightwork, a new grille (1955), and revised ''square'' engines (1952). It was during the life of the E type that Vauxhall Motors' output topped 100,000 vehicles per year for the first time, and the company produced its millionth vehicle. Compare the grille on this car with the earlier more American version shown elsewhere.

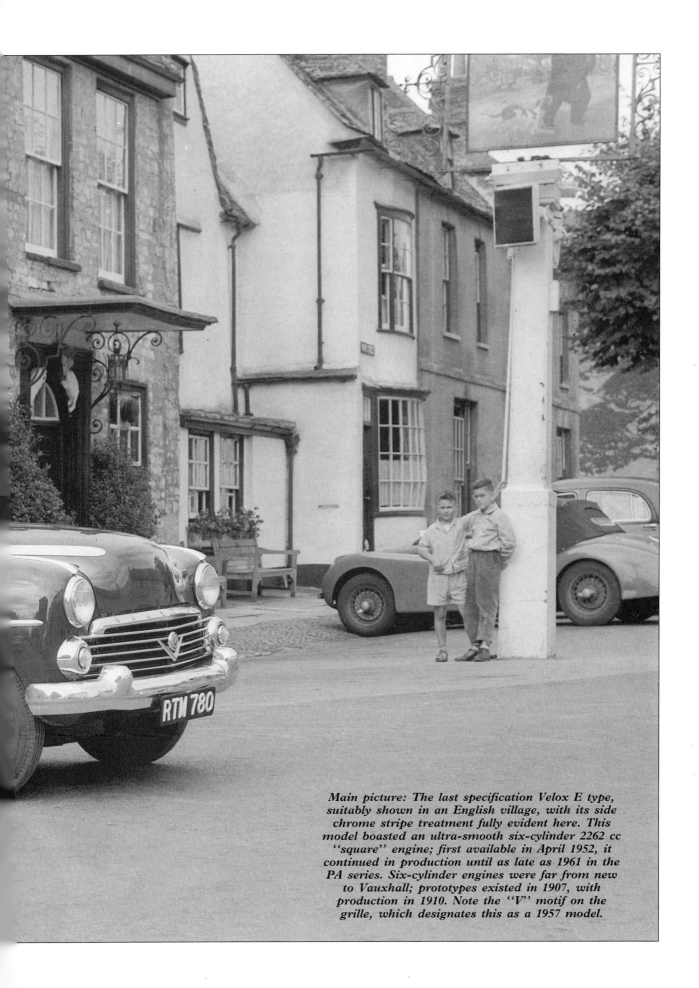

Main picture: The last specification Velox E type, suitably shown in an English village, with its side chrome stripe treatment fully evident here. This model boasted an ultra-smooth six-cylinder 2262 cc "square" engine; first available in April 1952, it continued in production until as late as 1961 in the PA series. Six-cylinder engines were far from new to Vauxhall; prototypes existed in 1907, with production in 1910. Note the "V" motif on the grille, which designates this as a 1957 model.

E types were certainly sold all over the globe, and all with the Vauxhall badge front and rear. This was before the days of crossbreeds and badge engineering! Of course some climates are kinder to cars than others. This photograph was taken in June 1990, in Christchurch, New Zealand, even though the setting looks rather English. Photograph: The Martin Cooper Collection.

Model	Engine	From	To
E TYPES			
Wyvern saloon	1442	8/51	4/52
Velox saloon	2275	8/51	4/52
Wyvern saloon	1507	4/52	early 57
Wyvern Grosvenor estate	1507	late 53	–
Velox saloon	2262	4/52	10/57
Cresta saloon	2262	10/54	10/57
Velox Grosvenor Swansong estate	2262	8/56	10/57
Velox Dormobile estate	2262	8/56	10/57

Note: Australian Holden E types also built as pick-up trucks and coupés

3

Velox, Cresta and Viscount — 1960s Luxury

The big, long, sleek PA sixes of 1957 confirmed to the beholder that, in styling them, Vauxhall had boldly moved closer to the contemporary American idiom, a trend first signalled with the introduction of the revolutionary Victor F some months earlier. Garish chrome, crazy colours, awesome tailfins (almost rivalling the Batmobile!), and plenty of character is possibly the best way to sum up the PA series, which actually became more Americanized as production continued. The Wyvern name had now departed for good (the Victor had plugged the four-cylinder model gap), leaving just the Velox and Cresta models with "square" 2.25-litre straight-six, new panoramic wrap-around windscreen, three rear windows, and later the Hydra-Matic transmission described elsewhere. Incidentally, Opel's counterpart was the Kapitän, of very similar appearance. Aesthetically, the panoramic windscreen looked much more more elegant on the Cresta; it was a little lower and a lot wider than the Victor F's — an interesting example of the effects of scale and proportion.

The engine was enlarged to 2.6 litres in 1960, a time when even bigger, more pronounced fins were added to the rear wing panels. Of course, these large Vauxhalls were not the only British cars to suffer "Atlantic drift". Humbers and Hillmans of the Rootes Group had panoramic windows, and Triumph Heralds had tailfins, as did the Ford six-cylinder models of the early 1960s. However, if any car should go down in history as American-influenced in this way, then it must surely be the PA — perhaps preserved in candy floss pink! A candy floss pink PA appeared on the cover of Lord Montagu's book *The British Motorist*. Many die-hard enthusiasts for the marque believe the PA to be one of the best-designed Vauxhalls ever to leave the factory. Even those who do not agree with this opinion must at least concede that it should go down as the most noticeable.

Friary Motors of Basingstoke built large capacity load-carrying estate conversions. A few crept through with the earlier grille design (of which only one seems to have survived). Most were produced with the "Phase 2" pattern from 1959. It was with the introduction of this grille (and the disappearance of the rear three windows) that the famous Vauxhall flutes were to disappear. These, of course, were not on the bonnet but on the body sides, as they had

THE NEW '61

The '61 Vauxhalls designed for the Motorway age are now in production. Here are the changes which make them even more attractive to own and drive.

VELOX

CRESTA

CRESTA AND VELOX: NEW 2.6 LITRE ENGINE

The new engine in the two 6-cylinder models gives truly masterful motoring. 113 brake horse power from a unit weighing only 45 lb. more than its 82 b.h.p. predecessor. Fabulous 'open-road' performance...effortless, high-speed cruising... remarkable top-gear traffic motoring...combined with outstanding economy. (Fewer revs per mile mean extra life and extra m.p.g.) New, more powerful brakes too. More stopping power. More resistance to fade. And new good looks—new colour schemes...new sealed beam headlamps...new instrument panel...new colour-changing moving-bar speedometer.

VICTOR: NEW FUNCTIONAL GOOD LOOKS

New, cleaner lines. New front end styling. New larger rear window. New instrument panel, colour schemes, detail finish. New padded facia in de Luxe models. And for extra long life at Motorway speeds, new high-duty big-end bearings for the famous Victor engine.

PLUS VAUXHALL QUALITY AND SAFETY

Superb road holding. Unequalled vision. All-synchro gears. Effortless steering and parking. Safe, powerful brakes. Complete underbody sealing.

Driving is believing. Make a date with your nearest Vauxhall dealer to try these splendid new cars. Find out for yourself that...

EVERYONE DRIVES BETTER

VAUXHALLS

UILT FOR THE MOTORWAY AGE!

VICTOR £510
+ £213.12.6 PT (£723.12.6)

VICTOR SUPER £535
+ £224.0.10 PT (£759.0.10)

VICTOR DE LUXE £565
+ £236.10.10 PT (£801.10.10)

VICTOR ESTATE CAR
£605 + £253.4.2 PT (£858.4.2)

VELOX 6-cylinder £655
+ £274.0.10 PT (£929.0.10)

CRESTA 6-cylinder £715
+ £299.0.10 PT (£1014.0.10)

VICTOR SUPER

A VAUXHALL

Vauxhall Motors Ltd · Luton · Beds.

been with the earlier Victor Fs. It would not be until the FE Transcontinentals appeared (perhaps the PAs were better qualified for this name tag than the humble FEs) that they made a surprising but welcome return — and to the bonnet again in an attractive V formation.

The PA made way in later 1962 for the more conservative and squarer-looking PB range of sixes, again the Velox and Cresta, with the almost obligatory estate conversion from an outside manufacturer, this time Martin Walter. From a distance the styling looked like that of the FB Victor, for it shared its doors

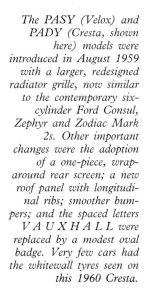

The PASY (Velox) and PADY (Cresta, shown here) models were introduced in August 1959 with a larger, redesigned radiator grille, now similar to the contemporary six-cylinder Ford Consul, Zephyr and Zodiac Mark 2s. Other important changes were the adoption of a one-piece, wrap-around rear screen; a new roof panel with longitudinal ribs; smoother bumpers; and the spaced letters V A U X H A L L were replaced by a modest oval badge. Very few cars had the whitewall tyres seen on this 1960 Cresta.

and sills with its smaller-bodied sister; but the PB was much wider and, of course, more powerful. The same 2.6-litre engine remained installed for a while, but it was replaced by a mammoth 3.3-litre cast-iron six pot in late 1964.

Interestingly, Vauxhall was celebrating record sales in 1964, with 342,873 cars and commercial vehicles sold. Illustrated in this chapter is the £1524 Radford Cresta conversion, which was the ultimate in comfortable cars, likely to be bought only by those lucky enough to have a chauffeur; perhaps you needed one to make use of the rear cocktail cabinet! Later-registered PBs can be identified by the later grille with its wider slats.

Exactly three years after the new PBs had been shown at the 1962 London Motor Show came the PCs. This time only the name Cresta appeared in the six-cylinder model brochures in standard and de luxe form. The Cresta was

Model	Cresta & Velox PA
Dates of Production	October 1957 to October 1962
Body Types	4-door saloon; estate conversion by Friary Motors of Basingstoke, from April 1959
Engines Offered	2262 cc, 6-cylinder (82 bhp); then 2650 cc, 6-cylinder (95 bhp)
Transmission	Manual: 3-speed with optional overdrive; or Hydra-Matic 2-speed auto transmission
Average Fuel Consumption	20 mpg (2.6-litre); 22 mpg (2.2-litre)
Top Speed	95 mph (2.6-litre); 89 mph (2.2-litre)
0-60 Mph	16.8 sec
Braking System	(Optional power assisted) front disc, rear drums
Wheels and Tyres	Wheels: 14 in; tyres: 5.90 x 14
Dimensions	Length: 15 ft; width: 5 ft 8¼ in; height: 4 ft 9 in
Weight	2765 lb (2.6-litre)
Production Changes	From September 1958 wider-opening front quarter lights, optional front centre armrests; Friary estate introduced, April 1959; from August 1960 larger grille and one-piece rear window
Price at Launch	£1073 17s 0d (Velox saloon) £1225 5s 0d (Velox estate) £983 17s 0d (Cresta)
Made at	Luton
Number Produced	173,759 PAs in total: 100,847 exported, 72,912 sold in UK; 1957-60: 81,841; 1960-2: 91,923
Chassis Identification	Velox PAS (from 1001): October 1957–August 1960 PADY (from 130,000): 8/1960-10/62 Cresta PAD: to August 1960 PADX: from August 1960 Last chassis no. 199,748

a fast car, especially in manual form (0 to 50 mph in 9.2 sec and a top speed of over 100 mph); police forces were keen customers, particularly of the estate conversion, again by Martin Walter, which made a splendid patrol car on Britain's new motorway network. Within a few months came the Viscount. As its name implies, this was the top-line model, with practically every conceivable contemporary gadget and extra fitted to it, including power-assisted steering and electric windows. The Viscounts and Crestas were lucky to make it to the summer of 1972, when production was discontinued for good. The FE Ventora was to continue the six-cylinder theme — although not for long.

This softly sprung 1961 PASX Velox saloon with its optional foglamps is pictured cornering hard while undergoing company trials. This car could well have had the optional Hydra-Matic three-speed transmission, available for some months on this model range. The reader should remember that automatic transmission was a rarity on any mass-produced car at this time. Vauxhall Motors' Sales Director said of the transmission "Wait till you get to know this new Hydra-Matic. Wait till you've driven a Cresta or Velox fitted with it along Oxford Street in the rush hour, or over a mountain pass. You'll find you're a complete convert.
That single, unified — and complete — control through your right foot, you'll find, gives you new pleasure in driving."

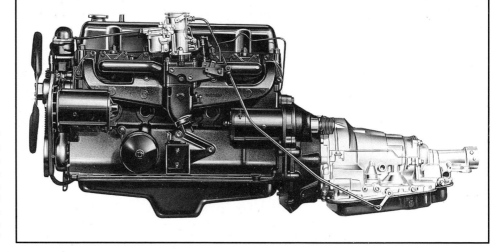

Here the PA's engine mass is clearly more than that of the gearbox, shown in this 1962 photograph. The length is due to the six-cylinder format, no doubt adding to the immense overall weight of the running gear!

Friary Motors Limited, of Basingstoke, offered a conversion on the PA chassis on both Velox and Cresta models, priced at £1222 and £1309 respectively from May 1959. These cars boasted an all-steel integral body with safety glass throughout, and could swallow 52 cu ft of luggage with the rear seat folded. Offered originally in eight two-tone colours (and just plain black), shortly afterwards extended to fifteen, the Friary was soon in big demand. According to the PA Owners Club, only 30 or so survive to date. Perhaps Vauxhall was quick to realize the great need for a dual-purpose car, for the Victor estate introduced soon afterwards was factory produced. The car photographed is a 1961 model with optional fog- and spotlamps. The earlier converted "three-window" types are rare — only one is known to have survived to date.

An early PA Cresta (denoted by the narrower grille treatment), pauses briefly while its entry number is cleaned during the 28th Monte Carlo Rally. Starting from the last lap are John Banks and C.G. Dunham, who set out from Glasgow. Note the bonnet straps, off-road tyres, triple spotlamps (with overhead integral hood), and windscreen fly trap on this otherwise standard-looking car. The numberplate is quite genuine, now no doubt worth thousands of pounds!

Earliest PAs had this rather peculiar bonnet badge mounted centrally toward the front. This was removed with the introduction of the revised grille (and disappearance of the "three-window" design) models featured earlier.

32

In 1962, some 13 months after the introduction of the Victor and VX 4/90 FB models, came the completely revised Cresta and Velox PB range, which replaced the five-year-old Cresta PAD and Velox PAS. American styling influences were much less noticeable — if at all. After a casual glance, the onlooker would have been forgiven for thinking he was looking at a contemporary Victor FB model. The somewhat wider PB shared the same door and sills, but here the similarity ends. At the top of this 1962 photo we see the Velox, and in the foreground is a Cresta identified by its more ornate wheel cappings, chrome body-side stripe and extra chrome work around the side windows. Has the gentleman two ladies in his life, or is the woman in the Velox just admiring his up-market Cresta?

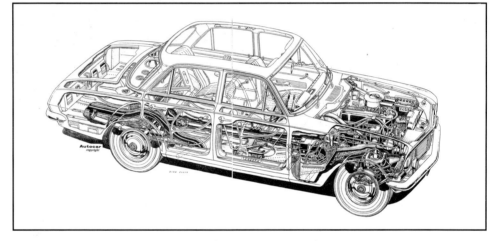

Model	Cresta & Velox PB
Dates of production	3 October 1962 to October 1965
Body Types	4-door saloon; 5-door estate conversion by Martin Walter from October 1963
Engines Offered	2651 cc (113 bhp); 3293 cc (128 bhp)
Transmission	Manual: 3-speed with optional overdrive; 4-speed, or Hydra-Matic transmission on 3.3-litre
Average Fuel Consumption	19 mpg
Top Speed	98 mph (3.3-litre); 92 mph (2.6-litre)
0-50 mph	10 sec
Braking System	Power brakes, front disc, rear drums
Wheels and Tyres	Wheels: 4.50 x 14; tyres: whitewall 5.90 x 14
Dimensions	Length: 15 ft 2 in; width 5 ft 10½ in; height 4 ft 8½ in
Weight	2700 lb (saloon) 2884 lb (estate)

Production changes	Radford conversion from October 1963; uprating of engines from October 1964, except for certain markets; optional 4-speed floor change at same time
Price at Launch	£936 (Velox); £1046 (Cresta)
Made at	Luton
Number Produced	87,044 PBs (includes Velox)

Above: *The Radford Cresta, for customers who needed that little extra on their top-of-the-range Vauxhall car. Harold Radford, already well known for his super de luxe version of the popular Mini, first displayed his luxury version of the Cresta at the 1963 London Motor Show. Among the exterior refinements were more ornate wheel cappings, a smart ribbed finishing strip was added to the back (later copied by the FD Ventora), extra lights on the C pillars, restyled front end with twin headlamps and new grille, painted strip beneath the existing chrome strip on the body sides, built-in reversing lights, front and rear overriders, and a special paint finish to the bodywork. Even more special attention was given to the interior. Lucky customers could boast folding tables hinged into the back of the front seats, adjustable reading lamps built into the roof; and the reclinable, height-adjustable seats, cubby hole and armrests were each trimmed in hide. A modified facia panel carried additional instrumentation with an all-transistor radio set with twin speakers and balancing control. Furthermore, the car came equipped with a sliding glass divider between the front and rear compartments — just right for holding conversations about the chauffeur's driving ability!*

Bottom and far left: *Late 1963 brought a load carrier, somewhat expensive for the day. This was the neat PB Cresta/Velox estate conversion by Martin Walter Ltd of Folkestone. It made use of fibreglass mouldings for the roof and rear hatch door, and offered 67 cu ft of luggage space, substantially more than look-alike FB Victor estates, thanks to its extra width. The load area floor was carpeted throughout, and chrome rubbing strips added protection when the car was in its dual-purpose role. Although the original Cresta/Velox rear lamp assemblies were used, the petrol filler cap was moved to the back of the vehicle, and the conversions had the "export" heavy-duty rear semi-elliptic leaf springs. As usual Vauxhall's full warranty was continued for the conversion.*

Insets: The name Velox finally lapsed when the PC models appeared at the 1965 London Motor Show. Initially it was the Cresta only, then the Viscount followed shortly, making the Cresta second rate for the first time in its history. Pictured here we see the Cresta De Luxe, easily distinguished by its twin headlamps and resulting narrower grille. Despite its apparent mass, the PC was actually an inch narrower than its immediate predecessor. The six-pot 3.3-litre power train was once again used — this unit (of American wartime origin) finally came to rest halfway through FE production. The author assumes this must be a pilot build test model the tax disc suggests this, with January 1966 as its expiry date. Note the unusual Griffin emblem mounted centrally on the bonnet.

Main picture: This 1964 Cresta PBDX was powered by the 3294 cc 128 bhp straight-six, unlike earlier (pre-October 1964) PBs equipped with the 2651 cc six-cylinder (the smaller unit was, however, continued for some export markets with high tax rates). Associated with engine enlargement was an optional four speed floor change, and revised rear axle gear ratios. Note the later grille.

Model	Cresta & Viscount PC
Dates of Production	October 1965 to summer 1972; Viscount from June 1966 to August 1972
Body Types	4-door saloon
Engines Offered	3294 cc (140 bhp)
Transmission	Manual, optional automatic; Powerglide to 1970
Average Fuel Consumption	20 mpg (manual)
Mpg at 56 mph	26 mpg (31 mpg with overdrive)
Top Speed	103 mph (manual)
0-50 Mph	9.2 sec
Braking System	Servo, front disc, rear drums
Wheels and Tyres	Wheels: $4\frac{1}{2}$J; tyres: 5.90 x 14
Dimensions	Length: 15 ft 7 in; width: 5 ft $9\frac{3}{4}$ in; height: 4 ft $9\frac{1}{2}$ in
Weight	2867 lb (Cresta)
	3080 lb (Viscount)
Production Changes	GM 3-speed auto replaced Powerglide, Autumn 1970
Price at Launch	£1058 17s 1d (Cresta De Luxe, November 1965)
	£1457 12s 1d (Viscount)
Made at	Luton
Number Produced	53,912 (Cresta)
	7025 (Viscount)

The public was treated to sumptuous carpets, armchair type seating, and a wooden dash shown for the first time in this Cresta PC example at the 1965 London Motor Show. Although mainly single-tone bodywork was offered on this model, the interior had a tasteful two-tone look, and door kick panels were given chrome embellishments and carpeting. Seen here is the standard three-speed automatic a four-speed manual box came as an option. The (slower) auto could still hasten the car along at 103 mph and give a respectable 0-60 mph time of around $12\frac{1}{2}$ seconds. The fuel consumption of this giant was a creditable 20 mpg.

Above left: By 1967, Martin Walter Ltd of Folkestone was back on the scene, having engineered this interesting, factory-approved estate conversion of the Cresta De Luxe. As with the PB conversion, many of the existing panels were used, including the rear lamp clusters. This model is certainly worth looking out for — very few seem to have survived the test of time. Normally they came in two-tone paint schemes. Note the rubber- (rather than chrome) surrounded rear side window, which gave it that "add on" look, also adopted much later by the Mark 1 Carlton estate. Photographs in the Vauxhall archives show police motorway patrol versions, although it is unclear how many were actually delivered in this form. *Above right:* By October 1970, the Viscount had the three-speed automatic GM gearbox fitted this time the lever was on the floor. Note the restyled dash layout and the deletion of the passenger's map reading lamp. No radio is seen here, although the speaker is visible, and was fitted as standard.

Enter the Viscount, basically an up-market variant of the established Cresta, introduced nine months earlier. Easily distinguished from its down-market cousin by its different grille and new vinyl-covered roof, the Viscount was so much more heavily equipped that it registered an extra 220 lb standing on the weighbridge. This quite understandably affected the 3.3-litre straight-six's performance; top speed was down 4 mph to 97 mph. Road testers of the day were impressed by the engine's overall smoothness and quietness; extra sound deadening had been added both under the bonnet, and with carpets. Wider-profile tyres improved the handling characteristics. Earlier models were equipped with a two-speed Powerglide transmission system, although a four-speed manual box could have been ordered with a saving of £85. By the autumn of 1970, the GM three-speed box had superseded the Powerglide. Note the chequered flag motif just visible below the wing-mounted Viscount badge, also found on the Brabham Viva (wing transfer), the VX 4/90 FD (dash) and the Royale coupé (tailgate).

Hydra-Matic (another word for "automatic") soon became a buzzword in the early 1960s, following Vauxhall's introduction of this super-smooth transmission system, adopted for the six-cylinder models. For the non-technically minded, the power arrives on the left, and departs at different speeds on the right!

Model	Engine	From	To
PA			
Cresta saloon	2262	10/57	8/59
Cresta estate (conversion)	2262	10/57	8/59
Cresta saloon (Mark 2)	2262	8/59	8/60
Cresta estate (Mark 2; conversion)	2262	8/59	8/60
Cresta saloon (Mark 2)	2651	8/60	9/62
Cresta estate (Mark 2; conversion)	2651	8/59	8/60
Velox saloon	2262	10/57	8/59
Velox estate (conversion)	2262	10/57	8/59
Velox saloon (Mark 2)	2262	8/59	8/60
Velox estate (Mark 2; conversion)	2262	8/59	8/60
Velox saloon (Mark 2)	2651	8/60	9/62
Velox estate (Mark 2; conversion)	2651	8/59	8/60
PB			
Cresta saloon	2651	10/62	10/64
Velox saloon	2651	10/62	10/64
Cresta estate	2651	10/62	10/64
Velox estate	2651	10/62	10/64
Radford Cresta	2651	10/63	–
Cresta saloon	3294	10/64	10/65
Velox saloon	3294	10/64	10/65
Cresta estate	3294	10/64	10/65
Velox estate	3294	10/64	10/65
PC			
Cresta saloon	3294	10/65	9/72
Cresta De Luxe saloon	3294	10/65	9/72
Cresta estate	3294	10/65	9/72
Viscount saloon	3294	6/66	8/72

Victors and Ventoras — Staid Family Transport

Totally new designs were a rarity in the 1950s, compared to the ever-proliferating examples from manufacturers today. One of the more interesting shapes to evolve in the 1950s was the original Victor, which made its début in March 1957. Showing obvious connections with designs from across the Atlantic (and indeed, the first prototype ran in Detroit in mid-October 1955) the all-new Victor Type F started a five-model, twenty-year saga for Vauxhall Motors.

Interesting is probably the appropriate word here, for the Victor Type F might be thought to look rather like one of those cartoon cars whose roof seemed to be travelling faster than the body! The concept of the wrap-around front and rear screens was well established in the United States — for some three years in fact — but was new to European eyes, and was soon copied by other manufacturers. Opel, for example, introduced its very similar Rekord (available in two-door form) with this window treatment. The feature was described enthusiastically by Vauxhall marketing as "panoramic windscreens" with "all-round vision". The front screen was inclined at 31°, which gave rise to a rather novel door design with a "dogleg" window pillar. A further talking point of the period was the displacement of the bonnet flutes, which had been a Vauxhall trademark, to the side of the vehicle (due to a shorter, lower bonnet).

Two models filled the new car showrooms: the Victor and the Victor Super. They were mechanically identical, but the Super sported several fittings and fixtures not seen on the basic model. These included armrests on all four doors, rear ashtray, two-note horn, door-activated courtesy light, an additional sun visor and a better steering wheel. Exterior enhancements were additional chrome side trim (indeed this stretched from the rear light surrounds and on to the rear doors, complete with the word "Super"), chrome window surrounds and an exhaust outlet through a "porthole" in the rear bumper. Vauxhall was not normally a company to offer gimmicks on its vehicles, and this latter feature was deleted only some 18 months into production. No doubt buying a new exhaust for an early Victor Super proved more difficult as time passed — rather reminiscent of today's owners of the rare Viva HB GT models having to convert to Magnum 2300 exhausts for the same reason.

Within a very short space of time the Victor F became Britain's number one export vehicle, which further emphasized the success of the new car. The Victor estate, something of an increasing rarity today, joined the fleet in March 1958. Mechanically it was identical to the saloon, the only noticeable difference in ride being a slight increase in noise. It was Vauxhall's first ever factory-produced estate — the first of many.

Stainless steel cappings were replaced on door pillars and side frames in September 1958, and by the end of the year the Victor 2 was introduced. This was basically the same vehicle, but was now available in three trim guises: Basic, Super and De Luxe. The last-named, the top of the range, had bucket seats. The new Victor 2 could be distinguished by its full-length radiator grille, a single bonnet ridge (there were previously two), wrap-around bumpers, smoother, simplified rear door treatment and oval side lights. It had now lost some of its signs of American influence and the gaudy circular caps on the ends of the bumpers (a so-called design feature) were deleted from the specification.

Final notable production changes to the Victor Type F were made in August 1960. By then the Super had earned itself attractive chrome cappings on the headlamp cowls, and all models were furnished with full-length side flutes with "Victor" on them, a deeper rear window and vertical flutes on the boot lid.

No gearbox or engine options were offered with the F type. The standard three-speed column-change box (now sadly only produced for some pick-up trucks) powered the vehicle up to 28 mph in first, 57 mph in second and to 76 mph in top gear. Vauxhall was keen to advertise the economy of the Victor on its launch and indeed an average of 30 mpg was significantly better than any of its serious rivals.

According to the early advertisements, using the all-synchromesh gearbox to hustle the car up to 50 mph took $14\frac{1}{2}$ seconds, although the *Autocar* recorded 18 seconds for this timed acceleration run on the early road test vehicle it examined. (Note that 0–50 mph used to be the standard acceleration measuring

run; the 0–60 mph was adopted at a later date as vehicles became both quicker and more refined.)

Over 330,000 examples of the Victor F were built. Although it is very much a rarity and memory today (sadly, most Type Fs lost their lives in the battle with corrosion), an active owners' club exists.

Late 1961 saw the arrival of the FB series, the second generation of Victors. Although these cars measured about the same as before, the styling was a vast improvement over the type Fs. The Victor no longer looked like a scaled-down caricature of a big flamboyant American car of the 1950s. The marketing department certainly made a point with the advertizing slogan:

> Good design means visual pleasure
> Good design means comfort
> Good design inspires confidence
> Good design means easy servicing
> Good design means good value

It all paid off, for nearly as many FBs were built in its three-year production run as there were of Type Fs in four years. Again, four-door saloons and a factory five-door estate car were offered in a choice of 14 colours; the latter had an attractive deep curved-at-the-top rear screen. Once again, there was a 1507 cc power unit, although this displacement was soon to increase. A three-speed column gearchange was a standard fitting as before, and all but the de luxe models had a bench front seat. Later models were fitted with a new larger front grille, this time in "rustproof" aluminium, and the front bumper height was raised at the same time in order to match the rear. Two-tone paintwork was still popular in this era: many surviving FBs retain this period feature. It seems that many more FB Victors have survived in the hands of enthusiasts than later, less interesting Type FC and FD models, which in any case had the disadvantage of selling in lower numbers.

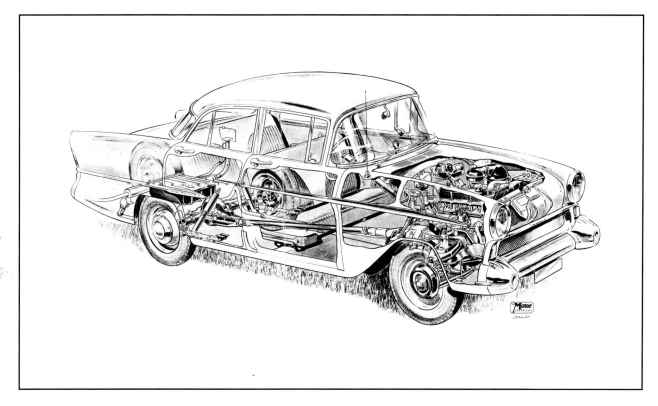

The 220,000 FC Victors, commonly known as the 101s, introduced the stylish "space curve" look. This added torsional strength — with associated improved handling — and gave them more than a passing resemblance to the contemporary PC Cresta and Viscount models. Compared to their predecessors these cars were slightly larger, with a good deal more space inside. Noticeable were the much slimmer window pillars. No big engine changes occurred during the three-year lifespan of the 101s. The 1594 cc engine was retained from the latest FBs, as was the three-speed gearbox with column change. Distinctive changes

Three Victors through the years (missing are the original Victor F and later FE). This photograph was in fact set up by the Vauxhall company itself in the late 1960s to demonstrate how Victor styling had changed. On the left stands a "facelifted" Victor FB Super; on the right a late model FC; in the foreground we see a "Coke bottle"-style Victor FD. Strangely, all three cars carry Vauxhall press vehicle registration numbers. Were they all part of a secret museum?

Model	Victor (Type F)
Dates of Production	March 1957 to July 1961
Body Types	4-door saloon; 5-door estate
Engines Offered	1507 cc
Transmission	3-speed manual
Average Fuel Consumption	30 mpg
Mpg at 56 mph	30 mpg
Top Speed	76 mph
0-50 Mph	18 sec
Braking System	Drums all round
Wheels and Tyres	Wheels: 13 in; tyres 5.60 x 13
Dimensions	Length: 13 ft 11 in; width: 5 ft 3 in; height: 4ft 10¾ in
Weight	2296 lb (saloon)
	2576 lb (estate)
Production Changes	Estate from March 1958; Series 2 from February 1959
Price at Launch	£728 17s (Base);
	£758 17s (Super)
Made at	Luton
Number Produced	390,745
Chassis Identification	FD Victor Super Saloon
	FE Victor De Luxe Saloon
	FS Victor Saloon (base model)
	FW Victor Estate

included extra side chrome towards the end of its production run, and a new front grille in 1967. The demise of the FC meant a sad goodbye to the trusty pushrod engine: the new FD used the slant four — the engine concept that lasted in car form to the 2.3-litre rally Chevettes.

The press was very good to the FD Victor after its announcement at the 1967 London Motor Show. Apart from becoming Car of the Show, the FD received the Don Safety Trophy. Even narrower pillars, and the introduction of a Viva style body swage beneath the window line, gave a crisp modern appearance to both the saloons and estates, none of which was available in the now rather dated two-tone colour combinations.

The Ventora was soon added to the FD range. Vauxhall stated that the all-coil-sprung car was intended for a straight-six unit from the outset — there certainly was more than enough room in the engine bay. The Ventora was called the "Lazy Fireball" by the Vauxhall marketing department, and easily out-sold the now rapidly ageing and cumbersome PC models, although it was not without its own shortcomings. For example, there was not even the option of reclinable front seats (well at least they were separate!) and many features that would normally be expected to be standard to a car of this calibre were, in fact, optional extras. This was put right in late 1969 with the Ventora II, introduced at the same time as a new version of the VX 4/90, and although performance suffered slightly because of detailed gearing changes, the model was more successful. The Victor slant fours (in 1600 and 2000 cc variants), the 3300 estate (basically a Ventora with comparatively more spartan Victor trim) and Ventora models continued virtually unchanged until, unusually, in early 1972, when the entirely new FE series were announced.

The Victor had been the backbone of Vauxhall cars since 1957. The FE, the last of a long series with this designation, was no exception. Called the

Above left: Part of the first consignment of Victor Fs bound for the USA for distribution by Pontiac Motor Division in 1957, shown here at the docks awaiting shipment; up to 2500 were soon being exported a month. These export models, all in left-hand-drive form, will have had their missing hub caps and wiper blades refitted (and, interestingly, interior mirrors) on arrival at their American dealers. The rust problems of these early model Victors may well have been less evident in the drier areas of the United States than they were on the home market. Visible are the twin bonnet flutes, mesh grilles, and large bumper end caps on these Series 1 Victors. In 1960 export of the four models of the Vauxhall Envoy to Canada started, essentially being a slightly modified Victor. On arrival in the United States some cars automatically had their roofs painted in tartan colours. The estate version for the US was known as the Vauxhall Envoy Sherwood. *Above right:* Even after a couple of years with the Enfield School of Motoring (North London), the Victor De Luxe (left) and Super (right) were in good shape! Approaching earliest F type Victors (1957-9) were instantly identified by the twin bonnet ridges, and large "dinner plate" caps on the ends of the bumper. Super models always carried a large quantity of chrome work, and on all but the last six months of the Series 1 Supers, the chrome was extended to the door window frames, as shown here.

"Transcontinental", the car was a far cry from original Victors of the late 1950s. The Victor FE, launched in February 1972, came from the same stable as two other new models in the FE range, the VX 4/90 and Ventora. The new model was both larger than any of its contemporaries, and more refreshing in its styling. Although the engines (albeit enlarged versions of the previous slant four overhead-cam units) were similar, the rest of the vehicle was largely a brand-new design, which somehow seemed to be much more up to date than its contemporaries, the 1970 Mark 3 Cortina and the 1971 Marina. Unlike Morris and Ford, however, Vauxhall offered no coupé. The company achieved what it had aimed to do: build a vehicle with increased interior dimensions, but not at the cost of taking up extra road space.

In common with the 1970 Viva HC estate, the FE estate — originally available in Victor form only (in 1800, 2300 and the rare 3300 engine forms) — sported a fastback-style rear window. This was a brave styling move at the time, made at the cost of removing a lot of rear luggage space when so much more might be expected in an estate based on a particularly big saloon, and when large rivals like the Volvo or Granada estates boasted more vertical rear screens. However, other manufacturers followed suit within the car's production life.

Apart from trim changes such as altering the grille background from silver to black, very little altered in Victor production in the mid-1970s. A limited

Left-hand-drive Series 2 Victor Fs for export being loaded to travel to port by rail. Such railway wagons could each carry six vehicles at a time. The two bottom cars were loaded first, and then ingeniously lowered by a series of pulleys, allowing room for four more cars on the top deck. Note the simplified, redesigned rear doors on these Series 2s.

production 2300S, marketed as a model in its own right, was exhibited at the London Motor Show in 1974 alongside Big Bertha, the Dealer Team Vauxhall Ventora 5-litre. The 2300S boasted a full luxury cloth interior, and distinctive coachwork and wheels.

Ventoras continued on in the guise of the FE, and were soon joined by a comparatively rare estate version that replaced the Victor 3300SL estate. These large, thirsty cars were the flagships of the Vauxhall range and were updated in 1974 for a fresher image. All Ventora saloons had vinyl-covered roofs and a limited edition Ventora VIP was available in black for a short while.

The Victors were replaced by the similarly styled VX 1800 and 2300 models, both in saloon and estate form, in early 1976. It was then that the Ventora was axed, which brought a sad close to Vauxhall six-cylinder motoring until the West German-engineered Royale models of October 1978. A 2300GLS was offered as a replacement for the Ventora, but all the FE series suffered bad sales from this point, due no doubt to the arrival of the Cortina/Taunus Mark 4, and of course its own Vauxhall stablemate the Cavalier Mark 1. By the summer of 1978 production (in Britain at least) had ceased and given way to the larger German-designed Carlton V cars. Today these Transcontinentals are still manufactured as far away as India, and sold as Hindustans. Here, remarkably, they are popular as taxis.

Certainly showing its 1950s origins is the interior of this Victor F. This one is an early Series 2, but with the Series 1 dash (worked out from the later door trims). This transition went on for 18 months, before a revised dash was introduced. Note the column-mounted gear-change. Reverse was towards the driver and up; first towards and down; second was forwards and up; and third (top) forwards and down.

By March 1958, in the last year of production of Series 1s, Victors were also offered in estate car form. The Victor estate was the first to be produced in volume in Britain. This model, a Series 2, was powered by a 1507 cc four-cylinder engine (later used in early FBs), and could take 45.5 cu ft of luggage. Differences from the saloon version (apart from obvious bodywork alterations) included heavier rate rear springs, wider tyres, higher axle ratio, heavier gauge axle tubes and larger hub bearings.

Potential owners could order their new load carriers in a choice of either five single colours or four two-tones. The cars were available with any of the saloon's optional extras — apart from the boot lamp.

Later in 1958 came the Newton drive transmission option — which made the Victor one of the first mass-produced automatics available in Britain.

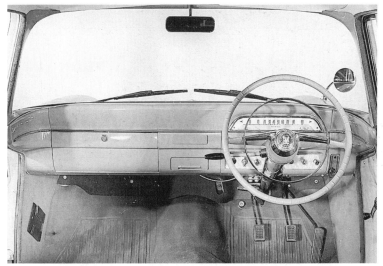

The clean line
of good design
and all the qualities of a fine car

THE NEW VAUXHALL VICTOR

Strangely, this revised dash layout on the F type Victor only lasted a year (August 1960 – September 1961). A completely new pressing had been manufactured, once again in metal to match the body colour. This time, instead of auxiliary switches dotted around the dash, each switch was placed on a chrome-backed facia in line with the steering column. The trend towards an arc-sweeping speedo arm continued, as did the column gearchange. Note the "Mercedes-style" wiper arm positioning shown here.

Very early FB days indeed, for this is a pre-production prototype Victor press vehicle, "somewhere in Wales" on evaluation. This car was more refined than the earlier F type, and certainly had a much less rust-prone body. Three-speed column change was standard, à four on the floor gearchange was an option. Four-door saloons in Standard, De Luxe and Super models and a factory-built estate made the line-up; power came from a straight-four 1507 cc engine. Shown here is a Super fitted with optional spotlamps (£3 17s 6d each) and wing mirrors (£1 17s 6d each). Other optional equipment was listed as individual front seats, a heater (!), screen washer, radio, safety belts and a rear anti-mist panel. So confident was Vauxhall with its new models that from March 1962 all new cars carried a full 12-month warranty.

Gentlemen of the press inspecting the all-new Victor FB in September 1961. Interestingly all the cars shown, which are registered with sequential Luton numberplates, were equipped with optional foglamps, this no doubt aiding the eager test drivers in the dark Welsh mountains at night. Car 106 ENM is displayed in two-tone bodywork, something that stayed popular on British cars until the mid- to late 1960s.

Model	Victor FB
Dates of Production	September 1961 to October 1964
Body Types	4-door saloon; 5-door estate
Engines Offered	1508 cc (49.5 bhp) or 1594 cc (58.5 bhp)
Transmission	3- or 4-speed manual
Average Fuel Consumption	1508 cc: 28 mpg
Mpg at 56 mph	1508 cc: 33 mpg
Top Speed	1508 cc: 76 mph
0-50 Mph	1594 cc: 12.7 sec
Braking System	Drums all round
Wheels and Tyres	Wheels: steel, $4\frac{1}{2}$J; tyres: 5.60 x 13
Dimensions	Length: 14 ft 5 in; width: 5 ft 4 in; height: 4 ft 9 in
Weight	2149 lb (saloon)
	2254 lb (estate)
Production Changes	Engine enlarged July 1963, plus larger brakes, and aluminium radiator grille; disc brakes optional
Price at Launch	£744 19s 9d (Standard)
	£781 8s 11d (Super)
	£847 1s 5d (De Luxe)
	£861 13s 1d (Estate)
Made at	Luton
Number Produced	328,640
Chassis Identification	FBD Victor Super Saloon
	FBE Victor De Luxe Saloon
	FBG Victor De Luxe Estate
	FBS Victor Standard Saloon
	FBW Victor Standard Estate

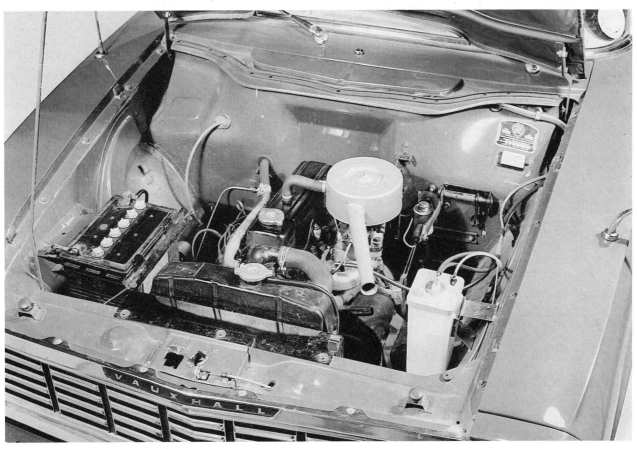

Above: Facelifted Victor FB, with revised power plant. The bhp was increased to 69 at 4800 rpm, while maximum torque came in at 2800 revs. A left-hand-drive model is featured here. Engines are not built like that any more!

Photographed in Vauxhall's own ground at Luton, an early FB Victor Estate De Luxe with two-tone coachwork. For the first time this estate looked like a properly designed car in its own right, rather than an afterthought or conversion as most previous models had done. This original three-speed FB model had a 1507 cc engine and could reach a somewhat noisy 76 mph.

The facelifted dashboard of a 1963 Victor FB estate, shown here in Super form. Revisions for 1963 included the repositioning of minor control knobs, so that a driver wearing the then optional safety belt could reach them. The presence of interior chrome and metalwork is fully evident here. Note the column gearchange, column-mounted handbrake, and horn ring mounted within the steering wheel. The FB was superseded by the less popular FC model in October 1964.

Above left: *The 1964 season brought a host of changes to the successful Victor FB models. The most notable alteration was to the front design shown here. A new corrosion-proofed anodized aluminium grille replaced the previous smaller unit, and the height of the front bumper was raised an inch to match the rear. The V A U X H A L L separate letter badging was removed from the leading edge of the bonnet and incorporated into the new grille design. Compare this to earlier photos, and note also that there was a third derivative of the FB grille on the VX4/90.* *Above right:* *A fine* concours *example of a 101 Victor of 1967. Examples like this in owners' clubs in Britain are common. Joining one of these clubs is almost essential for the owner of such a vehicle, for finding parts is increasingly a problem.*

A 1967 Victor 101 interior in top-of-the-line de luxe form shows optional inertia front and rear safety belts. The front seats (now separate) were comfortable, but lacked sufficient padding in the squabs. As displayed here, entry into the rear, where there was enough room for three adults, was easy, even for the elderly. Note the rear ashtrays incorporated into the combined door pull/armrest units. Not clearly visible is a front parcel shelf under the facia, with a lockable sliding door in the middle. The handsomely finished wood panel above was not made use of so as to allow more space.

Model	Victor 101 FC
Dates of Production	October 1964 to August 1967
Body Types	4-door saloon; 5-door estate
Engines Offered	1594 cc (70 or 76 bhp)
Transmission	Manual: 3-speed or optional 4-speed; or 2-speed automatic
Average Fuel Consumption	27 mpg
Mpg at 56 mph	30 mpg
Top Speed	81 mph
0-50 Mph	12.1 sec
Braking System	Drums all round; or optional power with front discs
Wheels and Tyres	Wheels: 4J, tyres: 5.60 x 13
Dimensions	Length: 14 ft 6¾ in; width: 5ft 4¾ in; height: 4ft 7¼ in
Weight	2316 lb (De Luxe Saloon)
Production Changes	September 1966: chrome side strip and new radiator added: engine bhp increased from 70 to 76; increase in compression ratio from 8.5:1 to 9:1; engines fitted with flexible flywheels, and other mechanical changes to the unit
Price at Launch	£678 (Standard)
	£708 (Super)
	£763 (De Luxe)
Made at	Luton
Number Produced	219,814

Late 1966 brought a slight style change to the 101 series for their last year in production. A sleeker, longer look was achieved by a restyled grille, and a narrow bright strip running the full length of the body. The Victor Super estate is portrayed here; the De Luxe (strangely more up-market than the Super) also featured a bright moulding along the sills. Also visible here are the taller-than-bonnet front wings, an unusual style not adopted on any other Vauxhall model.

Almost straight out of the Thames Television series Randall and Hopkirk (Deceased) *is this early white FD Victor saloon pictured in Denmark. Soon known as the "Coke bottle" (this design beat Ford's Mark III Cortina by three years), the FD Victor was awarded the* Don Safety Trophy *after its introduction at the London Motor Show in 1967. The* Times *called it Car of the Show, and the* Sunday Times *British Car of the Year. It is easy to see why when you compare the FD with photographs of the earlier FC 101 model.*

The original slant four, first used in the Randall & Hopkirk style FD Victors and VX 4/90s. "The 4-cylinder engine — available in 1.6- and 2-litre form — is test run under its own power before being installed", said the eager caption to this publicity photo. Note the obvious pancake air filter.

PXD 445F

Some six months after the introduction of the "Coke bottle" FD Victor (and certainly well before the delayed VX 4/90 FD), came wholly new luxury model with the comparatively lazy six-cylinder 3294 cc Viscount/Cresta engine. Easily distinguished by its harmonica grille, extra chrome work and standard black vinyl roof covering, the Ventora I weighed in at 2633 lb somewhat heavier than its four-cylinder sisters. No Ventora estate was ever offered in this guise, but a Victor 3300 estate emerged (later with the SL distinction added), albeit with a more spartan interior, but interestingly retaining that characteristic harmonica grille.

Model	Victor & Ventora FD
Dates of Production	October 1967 to March 1972 (Victor); March 1968 to March 1972 (Ventora)
Body Types	4-door saloon; 5-door estate
Engines Offered	1599 cc (80 bhp); 1975 cc (108 bhp); 3249 cc (140 bhp)
Transmission	Manual with optional overdrive; or automatic (on 1975 cc and 3294 cc models only)
Average Fuel Consumption	27 mpg (Victor); 20 mpg (Ventora)
Mpg at 56 mph	34 mpg (Victor); 27 mpg (Ventora)
Top Speed	89 mph (Victor); 103 mph (Ventora I); 106 mph (Ventora II)
0-60 Mph	18.3 sec (Victor 1600); 15 sec (Victor 2000); 11.8 sec (Ventora I)
Braking System	Servo, front discs, rear drums
Wheels and Tyres	Wheels: $4\frac{1}{2}$J x 13; tyres 560 x 13 cross-ply; Ventora 165 x 13 radial
Dimensions	Length: 14 ft $8\frac{3}{4}$ in; width: 5 ft 7 in; height: 4 ft 4 in
Weight	2352 lb (1600 saloon) 2386 lb (2000 saloon) 2352 lb (2000 estate: auto) 2633 lb (Ventora)
Production Changes	May 1968: introduction of estates; January 1970: GM automatic transmission option, and the Victor Super, superseded the Basic model; Ventora 2 introduced October 1969
Price at Launch	£819 2s 4d (Victor 1600) £910 1s 6d (Victor 2000) £1101 (Ventora)
Made at	Luton
Number Produced	198,085 (including Ventora)

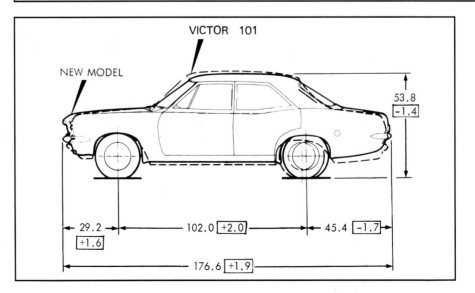

Space curve out, "Coke bottle" in Vauxhall artist's view on how the FC Victor (dotted) compared to the longer, lower and sleeker FD model.

4/38

By the early 1970s all Vauxhall estate cars were produced by the factory, and not converted by outside firms as was done previously in many cases. A 1971 Victor 2000SL estate, shown here, could take in 60.5 cu ft of luggage through its top-hinged tailgate. The slant four could have been ditched in favour of a straight six in this guise; the 3.3-litre Ventora unit was offered in the 3300SL estate, identified at the front by the Ventora grille and at the rear by twin exhaust outlets. This press photograph would have been issued a few months before the launch of the FE series.

Coinciding with the launch of the VX 4/90 FD, the Ventora was facelifted — and the Ventora II was born. There were many revisions and additions compared with the previous model. The new car shared its redesigned interior with the VX 4/90. The plain rear bench seat was replaced by a luxury two-seater unit; the front seats were reclinable (not even an option before); reversing lamps were added to the specification, as was a heated rear window; there was a higher final drive ratio, allowing a slightly increased top speed (103 to 106 mph) at the cost of acceleration but giving better fuel consumption. Fitting a large engine into a small body (which had become a trend with many manufacturers by the late 1960s) had some alarming side effects. One Autocar tester reported "It is quite easy to spin the rear wheels during a hard standing start, because of the relatively low proportion of the overall weight which they carry." The tyres, incidentally, were still cross-plies 6.9 x 13 in.

Main picture: The 1970/71 season "J" registration tells us that this is a pre-production Victor saloon undergoing trials, no doubt at Millbrook. Components readily get swapped about on evaluation models, and this vehicle is no exception this Victor has Ventora wheels. The lack of tax disc compels us to question whether the vehicle was eventually sold off or scrapped as a well-used test vehicle. The ill-fitting bonnet and front spoiler panel certainly prove the prototype point. Note the oddly situated interior mirror and obvious lack of side badge.

Bottom right inset: October 1969 brought the introduction of a better automatic transmission system for all models, shown here in this splendid diagram drawn by GM in Europe. This introduced smoother and more efficient operation. Note the detachable torque converter housing, allowing the gearbox maximum compatibility.

Below inset: Although spartan by today's standards, the interior of a 1970 Ventora II (FD) was certainly lavish at the time. The Ventora II brought a new range of upholstery colours (which colour-keyed the headlining). Headrests were a long way off at this stage eight years for Vauxhall, becoming available with all V car models initially, then slowly across the range. Luton's sales slogan was the Lazy Fireball *and the boast was "Long striding luxury of the open road, plus lazy top gear flexibility".*

Detachable torque converter housing

Input shaft

Concentric clutch packs

Output shaft

Parking lock pawl

Valve body

Oil pump

Selector mechanism

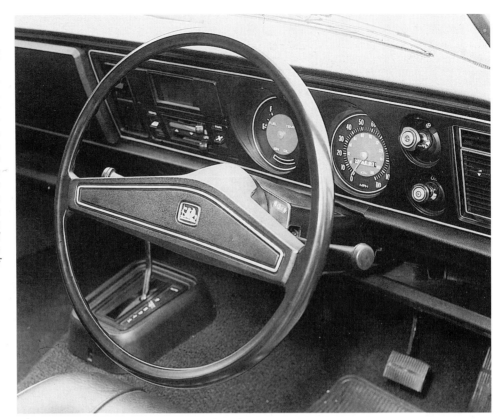

The original all-black (and rather "plasticky") facia from a Victor 1800 automatic appears quite spartan by today's standards. The 2300 model had a rather cheap-looking wooden veneer finish to both the dashboard itself, and the centre piece of the steering wheel. The knobs shown to the right control the lights and the choke. Note again the early 1970s trend to slope the dash down and away from the driver, also evident on the earliest of the Mark 3 Cortinas.

Spring 1972 meant a fresh series of Victors, called the Transcontinentals, *and in turn the VX 4/90 and Ventoras were brought up to date. As there were no plans for a replacement model for the seven-year-old Crestas and Viscounts, it became increasingly more important to make the Ventora that little bit more different from its Victor sisters; it was very soon to become the top Vauxhall model. This was achieved by once again utilizing that lazy cast-iron straight-six 3.3-litre engine (the origins of which dated back to Chevrolet in wartime), and subtly changing a whole host of detail components. The roof was vinyl covered (as on the FDs, although the roof of the rare Ventora estate of 1973 remained uncovered), waist level rubbing strips were added, and the wheels were enlarged to 14 in. Wood veneer was featured on the dashboard, and more lavish seats and door trims were employed. Perhaps one of the more striking features was the rather large, centrally mounted griffin on the front grille. In 1973 came a very special limited edition so rare now, the author wonders if any have survived. Enter the Ventora VIP an all-black super-luxury version, no doubt aimed at company directors of the day.*

Model	Victor, Ventora & VX (FE)
Dates of Production	March 1972 to January 1976 (Victor & Ventora); January 1976 to summer 1978 (VX)
Body Types	4-door saloon; 5-door estate
Engines Offered	1759 cc (77 bhp); 2279 cc (100 bhp); 3294 cc (124 bhp)
Transmission	4-speed manual; optional 3-speed automatic
Average Fuel Consumption	23 mpg (1800); 22 mpg (2300); 20 mpg (Ventora)
Mpg at 56 mph	27 mpg (1800); 31 mpg (2300); 24 mpg (Ventora)
Top Speed	89 mph (1800); 96 mph (2300); 102 mph (Ventora); 104 mph (VX 2300)
0-60 Mph	17.3 sec (1800); 12.4 sec (2300); 12.6 sec (Ventora)
Braking System	Dual circuit, servo-assisted, front disc, rear drums
Wheels and Tyres	Wheels: 5J x 13 in; tyres: 175SR x 13 radial Ventora: Wheels 6J x 14 in; tyres 185/70 x 14 radial
Dimensions	Length: 14 ft $10\frac{4}{5}$ in; width: 5 ft $6\frac{9}{10}$ in; height: 4 ft $5\frac{9}{10}$ in
Weight	2499 lb (1800 saloon)
	2572 lb (1800 estate)
	2552 lb (2300 saloon)
	2689 lb (2300 estate)
	2651 lb (Ventora saloon)
Production Changes	September 1972: 1800 Super front bench seat replaced by separate units, and 2300 Super deleted from range; October 1973: 3300 SL estate discontinued; front grille on 1800 painted black from 1973; Ventora estate from October 1973
Price at Launch	£1299 (2300 SL) £2991 (VX2300)
Made at	Luton
Number Produced	44,078 (Victor 1800/2300)
	693 (Victor 3300 Estate)
	7291 (Ventora)
	25,815 (VX 1800/2300)

A rare classic for the future? This picture has been chosen carefully and deliberately this car could quite easily be swallowed up in automotive history and forgotten. It was the most potent production Victor ever. Look carefully at that badge 3300SL! As the twin exhaust outlets prove, the 3300SL Victor FE estate followed in the footsteps of the 3300 FD, but had lasted in production for just over a year when replaced by the Ventora estate, introduced in October 1973. This variant of the Victor was never a big seller; the author has seen only one roadgoing example. Its extra thirst and limited extra available power (from what was basically an engine dating back to the Second World War), coupled with handling characteristics made worse by the heavy cast-iron power unit (particularly evident on winding roads), usually resulted in potential customers buying the less exciting 2300SL estate. Outwardly, the extra power was not immediately obvious, except from the extra exhaust outlet, larger Ventora wheels and, of course, badge (rear only). Six-cylinder FE Victors shared the grilles of their smaller-engined sisters; FD Victor sixes had the harmonica grille of the Ventora.

Although this rear-end photograph highlights just how basic the Victor 1800 saloon appeared, it is easy to overlook how modern the Transcontinental design was for the early 1970s. Compared to a Cortina Mark 3, for example, the FE series appeared much sleeker, but unfortunately the sluggish 1800 and 2300 engines could not quite match the performance of the smaller-engined Fords. The 2300 Victor saloon and estates had a metal capping between the rear lamp units, bordered top and bottom by chrome strips. The Griffin emblem against a plain painted background shown here was exchanged for the name Vauxhall within a stainless steel strip. This strip was static on the saloons, but lifted as part of the tailgate on estate models.

The attractive chrome window surrounds and blackened wheel centres suggest this is a Victor 2300SL saloon of about 1973. Unfortunately, as popular as the car was, it was never sold in such large numbers as the Ford Cortina Mark 3 despite having a two-year edge over the latter in design. The large overhead cam in-line four-cylinder engine — probably the largest British four-cylinder unit on the market — had an output of 100 bhp. Top speed was a modest 96 mph; fuel consumption ranged in the mid-20s. Note the return of those once traditional bonnet flutes, not seen on a new Vauxhall for a decade and a half, since removed from the first PA Velox/Cresta series. Note, too, that the floorpan of the FE was identical to that of its German Commodore cousin models.

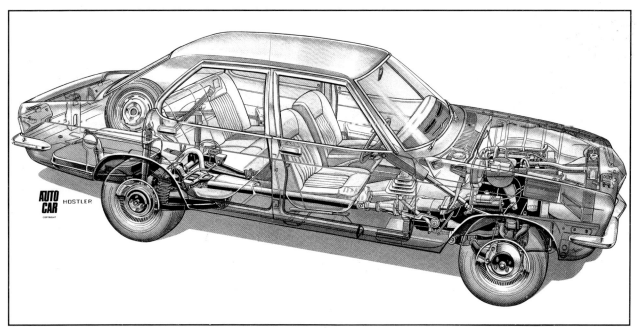

64

Top: *Despite popular belief, the Vauxhall 2300S was a very rare model in its own right and certainly not part of the regular Victor range of models. To all intents and purposes, however, the 2300S Limited Edition was an uprated Victor 2300SL saloon without the badges! Usually finished in metallic light blue (although there was the option of green), and always with smart twin coachlines, the 2300S aimed to have an exclusive look aided by a black vinyl roof covering (a kit was optional on the Victor), door-mounted mirrors, black wheels with chrome wheel trims, chrome wheel arch treatment "borrowed" from the contemporary VX 4/90 and Ventora FEs, and a full colour-matched cloth interior. The "S" distinction was made by a modest red transfer badge to the right of the chrome 2300 badge on the boot lid. Preceding the Chevette by five months, the new 2300S was first shown at the 1974 London Motor Show.*

Middle and bottom: *Unlike its contemporary sisters in the Vauxhall line-up, the 2300S boasted colour-keyed brushed nylon trim, and a central armrest in the rear seat. A radio with mono cassette player was standard equipment. Note that despite these luxury offerings, headrests had still not been introduced on any Vauxhall car. Also lacking here were power-operated windows unusual since the top line Viscount (by now discontinued) had been fitted with these since 1966!*

Above left: The 58 cu ft available in an FE estate — this one in the luxury guise of a 1974 Ventora. Compare this picture with the 1972 example; the chrome trims at the bottom of the side panels are gone, wiper blades and arms are now black, and there are rubber moulding strips on the bumpers. Note that the standard equipment vinyl roof of the saloon was not carried on to the estate models. While writing this book, the author was lucky enough to test-drive a rare 3300 cc Ventora estate and can reveal that, although it was in automatic form, it certainly was not slow! Above right: The VX 1800 and 2300 replaced the ubiquitous Victor model in January 1976. Here we see the humble VX 1800. Detail styling changes included larger, now halogen headlamp/indicator units; a larger grille (visually achieved by having the chrome capping open with the bonnet, unlike the earlier Victors — BMC performed the same successful operation with the Mark 2 Mini); and new wooden facia and centre console. Both models boasted chrome window surrounds (not on previous 1800 Victors) and coachline treatment. The VX 1800 and 2300 were identical, save for badging; only an underside inspection would reveal a rear anti-roll bar on the 2300. The fastback estate continued in this new guise. Unusually the ribbed velour upholstery of the saloons was not fitted in the estates at first — ambla trim was all that was available, until March 1977 when ribbed velour was put in across the range, making the saloon and estate specification virtually identical. The VX series was not a success and production ceased in the summer of 1978, when the Luton lines were cleared for the forthcoming Carlton.

Vauxhall's flagship of the range from 1976 was the executive 2300GLS — the first top of the range Vauxhall for very many years not to be six-cylinder-powered. This car replaced the ageing Ventora and boasted a whole host of improvements. Besides the fresh new colours, new interior trim, a new grille, chrome sill cappings, and dashboard were among the improvements. The addition of the good-looking front spoiler improved both the mpg (much needed with the FEs, especially when compared to the new Cavalier 1 of late 1975) and top speed. "Extra dark wine" both complemented the vinyl roof and gave the model an exclusive look, for this colour was only available with the VX 2300GLS. Other standard equipment included a rev counter, power steering, halogen lights, and even rear-door-operated courtesy lights.

Big Bertha *was the nick-name given to perhaps one of the most famous of Dealer Team Vauxhall's cars. Shown here at the 1974 London Motor Show, the 5-litre V8-engined supercar was a real crowd puller. Providing 495 bhp at 7600 rpm, the Ventora lookalike was geared for a top speed of almost 160 mph. Sadly, the vehicle's racing career lasted for only six months on the track; it crashed heavily in a Silverstone race at 100 mph, and although the engine lived on in DTV's next adventure — Baby Bertha (the Firenza) — the bodywork was scrapped. Fortunately, driver Gerry Marshall was not hurt.*

Vauxhalls and Vespas! While this book was being compiled there were many sources indicating that the Transcontinental FE series was still in production in India. Research has proved that it is. This new Hindustan, looking for all the world like a VX 1800 saloon, was snapped in Delhi in late 1989. Photograph The Martin Cooper Collection.

Model	Engine	From	To
F			
Victor saloon Series 1	1507	3/57	1/59
Victor Super saloon Series 1	1507	3/57	1/59
Victor estate Series 1	1507	3/58	1/59
Victor saloon Series 2	1507	2/59	9/61
Victor Super saloon Series 2	1507	2/59	9/61
Victor De Luxe saloon Series 2	1507	2/59	9/61
Victor estate Series 2	1507	2/59	9/61

FB

Victor Standard saloon	1507	9/61	10/64
Victor Standard estate	1507	9/61	10/64
Victor Super saloon	1507	9/61	10/64
Victor De Luxe saloon	1507	9/61	10/64
Victor De Luxe estate	1507	9/61	10/64

FC

Victor 101 saloon	1594	10/64	9/67
Victor 101 Super saloon	1594	10/64	9/67
Victor 101 De Luxe saloon	1594	10/64	9/67
Victor 101 Super estate	1594	10/64	9/67
Victor 101 De Luxe estate	1594	10/64	9/67

FD

Victor 1600 saloon	1599	10/67	10/69
Victor 2000 saloon	1975	10/67	10/69
Victor 1600 estate	1599	5/68	10/69
Victor 2000 estate	1975	5/68	10/69
Victor 3300 estate	3294	5/68	10/69
Victor 1600 Super saloon	1599	10/69	2/72
Victor 1600 Super estate	1599	10/69	2/72
Victor 2000 Super saloon	1975	10/69	2/72
Victor 2000 Super estate	1975	10/69	2/72
Victor 2000 SL saloon	1975	10/69	2/72
Victor 2000 SL estate	1975	10/69	2/72
Victor 3300 SL estate	3294	10/69	2/72
Ventora	3294	2/68	10/69
Ventora II	3294	10/69	2/72

FE

Victor 1800	1759	3/72	1/76
Victor 1800 estate	1759	3/72	1/76
Victor 2300SL	2279	3/72	1/76
Victor 2300SL estate	2279	3/72	1/76
Victor 3300SL estate	3294	3/72	9/73
2300S Limited Edition	2279	10/74	–
Ventora	3294	3/72	1/76
Ventora VIP Limited Edition	3294	1973	–
Ventora estate	3294	9/73	1/76
VX 1800	1759	1/76	10/78
VX 1800 estate	1759	1/76	10/78
VX 2300	2279	1/76	10/78
VX 2300 estate	2279	1/76	10/78
VX 2300 GLS	2279	1/76	10/78

5

The Sporting VX 4/90s

The VX 4/90 story started with the introduction of the Victor FB models —
or one month later in October 1961 to be precise. The new model, badged
VX four ninety (spelled out), was the first specifically high-performance product
since the famous 30/98, with particular appeal to keen drivers with no time
to waste. Easily distinguished by its different radiator grille treatment, decorative colour flashes along the body flanks, rearrangement of tail lamps, and additional polished aluminium wheel trims, the FB VX four ninety was an amazing
44 per cent more powerful than contemporary Victor saloons. This was brought
about by the use of a light alloy cylinder head, fed by twin Zenith carburettors. Naturally, models were equipped with extra instrumentation, whilst separate
front seats, folding rear seat armrests and wood-grained dash added that touch
of luxury.

Despite the public announcement in October 1961, production only started
in late January 1962. By 7 September that year, the 10,000th car had rolled
off the production line; 3500 of them had gone overseas.

The 101 FC curved windowed Victors were announced at the 1964 London
Motor Show, and alongside was a wholly new high-performance VX 4/90 version, complete with obligatory side strip in a contrasting colour, wheel dec-
oration and superior front grille. Now easily capable of over 90 mph, the 74
bhp (later 81 bhp) vehicle had power brakes (front disc, rear drum) as standard and, like the earlier FB version, a four-speed floor-mounted gearshift. Some
13,449 FC VX 4/90 cars were produced in the model's three-year life. As with
all VX 4/90s, no trim or body options were ever made available.

Unfortunately, when the FC range was replaced by the much superior "Coke
bottle" FDs in 1967, it looked as though it was the end of the road for the
VX 4/90. This was because no VX 4/90 was made available in the new FD
guise, and it was not until the Paris Motor Show late in 1969 that a surprised
public saw the reintroduction of this sporty model. Now with the familiar white
cross treatment on the front grille, the FD version was bigger than ever, and
had 112 bhp on tap from its willing slant four 1975 cc engine. It could just
attain (and only just!) 100 mph. Eager first customers had to wait several months
before deliveries started; a combination of component and labour problems at

the factory caused this but, within two years, 14,277 of the FD VX 4/90s had rolled off the production lines.

In the spring of 1972, the FE VX 4/90 made part of the new FE line up, and once again sported the distinctive white cross, this time on the FE's attractive squarer, deeper profile grille. Once again Rostyle wheels were the order of the day, and another increase in capacity brought this version of the VX 4/90 up to 2279 cc, in line with the new Victor cars. Few modifications (apart from cosmetic, colour and dashboard changes) were made to the car and once again the VX 4/90 disappeared from the brochures, this coinciding with the introduction of the VX 1800/2300 models. Just to confuse the issue, however, the FE VX 490 (no oblique this time) came back again to make a brief, very

Before the introduction of the FC, this FB model's designation had been changed to VX 4/90. This can be easily explained VX stands for Vauxhall, four details the number of cylinders, and 90 was the term the company gave to more powerful versions of a model. The car is displayed on a motor show stand. Despite a slight curvature in the body, the side glass was still straight; this of course was changed when the FC Vauxhall bodies arrived.

Model	VX 4/90 FB
Dates of Production	February 1962 to October 1964
Body Types	4-door saloon
Engines Offered	1507 cc (70 bhp); then 1594 cc (73 then 81 bhp)
Transmission	4-speed manual
Average Fuel Consumption	23 mpg
Mpg at 56 mph	33 mpg
Top Speed	88 mph
0-50 Mph	10.3 sec
Braking System	Front disc, rear drums
Wheels and Tyres	Wheels: 14 in; tyres 5.60 x 14.4 ply
Dimensions	Length: 14 ft 5¾ in; width: 5 ft 4 in; height: 4ft 9½ in
Weight	2100 lb
Production Changes	July 1963: larger engine fitted
Price at Launch	£971 0s 7d
Made at	Luton
Number Produced	N/A
Chassis Identification	FBH

low-volume production run, this time with the German Getrag 5-speed gear-box and in much livelier form. Around 900 were produced, all in manual form. 200 left hookers went to Sweden and 20 went to the Spanish police. This final model went with the rest of the FEs in summer 1978 to make way for the new Carltons. A proposed fuel-injected VX 490E never made production.

Worthy of mention here is the later Viceroy, which was also adorned with the white cross on its front grille, although not related to the VX 4/90 range in any shape or form. Coincidentally, this model was the more powerful version of the company's bread-and-butter saloon (in this case the Carlton), just as the VX 4/90 was in relation to the Victor.

Has the gentleman wearing the driving gloves realized this particularly early VX four ninety has left-hand drive? Clearly a well-posed publicity photograph of the new VX four ninety the car for the family man with places to go. This early VX four ninety lacks the rear numberplate sur-round (which only allowed a square plate to be fitted) found on later FBs. You needed an acquired taste to approve of the extra verti-cal rear lamp fittings found on this model. Note, too, the lack of heated rear window, and superfluous chrome embellishments on the boot lid and the interior of the door. Within nine months of the start of production, no fewer than 3500 of the 10,000 VX four nineties produced had gone overseas to 80 different countries.

One of the first VX 4/90s built, a 1961 "VX four ninety" FB pauses for pho-tography in rural England. In its standard twin carb form, it was good for 90 mph — creditable and legal, at least on a motor-way, if you could find one — although less than 20 mpg was the penalty here; and it even gave the earliest Austin and Morris 998 cc Mini Coopers a run for their money. Both FB and FC VX 4/90s had contrasting coloured coach-lines. Note the rear foglamps, a factory optional then, but eventually made a legally required fitting on all cars registered in the United Kingdom after 1979.

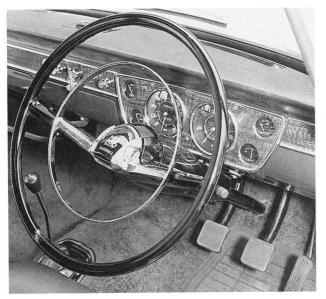

Above left: *Unlike more modern VX 4/90s, wood panelling on this early FB facia was the order of the day. Even at the early stage a rev counter was standard equipment, confirming the car's sporty appeal, along with water temperature, ampmeter, and oil pressure gauges. Just like its Victor sister, the large chromium ring inside the steering wheel was in fact the horn. Note that despite being brand new, the indicator warning bulb (mounted centrally between the rev counter and speedo) is already missing!*

Above right: *A new model Victor meant a new VX 4/90. Here we see a new 1966 VX 4/90 FC highlighting the special rear tail lamp treatment reserved for such a model. Compare these to its contemporary cousin, the Victor FC. Note too the additional chrome-surrounded side flash. Standard features included a limited slip differential (from 1966), flasher hub caps, and a 90 mph, 85 bhp engine. Earliest FC versions sported a VX 4/90 badge on the upper rear quarter panels. Second generation models (as this left-hand-drive version is) had additional chrome work along the body flanks, and the aforementioned side motifs repositioned nearer to the back lights. No estate version was ever offered with any model in the VX 4/90 range. Very few of the FC type VX 4/90s seem to have survived the test of time.*

Model	VX 4/90 FC
Dates of Production	October 1964 to August 1967
Body Types	4-door saloon
Engines Offered	1594 cc (74/81 bhp)
Transmission	4-speed manual; or 2-speed automatic
Average Fuel Consumption	22 mpg
Mpg at 56 mph	32 mpg
Top Speed	90 mph
0-60 Mph	16.0 sec
Braking System	Power brakes, front discs, rear drums
Wheels and Tyres	Wheels: 4J; tyres: 5.60 x 13
Dimensions	Length: 14 ft 8¾ in; width: 5 ft 5¼ in; height: 4 ft 7½ in
Weight	2218 lb
Production Changes	September 1966: chrome side stripe added, engine bhp increased from 74 to 81 bhp, and increased compression ratio; plus other mechanical changes to engine
Price at Launch	£872
Made at	Luton
Number Produced	13,449
Notes	Has limited slip differential, side colour flash

Above left: *The grille remained the same as the one shown here in a different view of the same Mark 2 FC VX 4/90. The most striking point to the casual contemporary onlooker would have been the pronounced curvature of the body sides. More interior comfort, coupled with the resulting stronger panels from the "space curve" as it was known, heralded a new start in motoring history. The space curve factor alone practically doubled torsional stiffness and led to greater structural safety, and quieter tauter characteristics, making this a more refined car on the open road. In all, some 13,449 units such as the one pictured here were built in the three-year production run. When the FD model was announced at the 1967 London Motor Show, the VX 4/90 name disappeared from the Vauxhall range, at least for a while.* **Above right:** *Just as the Hydra-Matic had taken off half a decade earlier, the Powerglide automatic transmission from Vauxhall became an important trademark from 1965. This particular unit was used in the Victor and VX 4/90 FC models. Note the unit's compactness, and the 10 in diameter torque converter.*

Paris October 1969 the 112 bhp VX 4/90 FD was officially unveiled at the French Motor Show. Only a handful of press cars were produced at first a combination of component and labour problems at the factory meant there were no deliveries to enthusiastic owners until February 1970. Some 14,277 VX 4/90 FD models were completed in its limited 24-month production run; a creditable 137 averaged per five-day week. Note that the V A U X H A L L badging displayed on earlier FB/FC VX 4/90 types had now been replaced by this attractive white cross, later carried on to FE VX 4/90s and the later (V car) Viceroy. Near 100 mph performance (it almost kept up with the lighter, similarly engined Viva GT) on such a heavy car was at the cost of petrol consumption 21 mpg was average.

Model	VX 4/90 FD
Dates of Production	October 1969 to March 1972
Body Types	4-door saloon
Engines Offered	1975 cc (112 bhp)
Transmission	Manual with standard overdrive; optional automatic
Average Fuel Consumption	21 mpg
Mpg at 56 mph	28 mpg (overdrive: 32 mpg)
Top Speed	97 mph
0-60 Mph	13.2 sec
Braking System	Servo, front disc, rear drums
Wheels and Tyres	Wheels: Rostyle 5.0; tyres: 6.9 x 13 low profile cross-ply (radial optional)
Dimensions	Length: 14 ft 8¾ in; width: 5 ft 7 in; height: 4 ft 4 in
Weight	2486 lb
Price at Launch	£1203 8s 1d
Made at	Luton
Number Produced	14,277
Notes	Scheduled availability for November 1969, actually February 1970 due to component/labour problems at Vauxhall factory

Below left: According to the press office in 1970, the VX 4/90 FD interior had "special appeal for the fast cruising, long distance driver". Perhaps by that they meant that a rev counter, oil pressure gauge, ampmeter, and water temperature gauges were all available for inspection by this enthusiastic motorist. Just visible here is the overdrive select control housed on the top of the gear lever (not available with the much rarer automatic model). This single feature boosted fuel consumption by about 4 mpg on a steady run. Note also the leather-rimmed steering wheel and full deep pile carpeting. Below right: The 112 bhp 2-litre slant four in twin carb form had been only available in the Viva GT. Enter the new VX 4/90 after its first of two periods of non-existence. For maximum performance, the engine was allied to a specially designed air cleaner and exhaust system that was new from the manifold through to the bright-finished tailpipe sleeve.

One of the original three different fronts offered on the attractive Transcontinental FE range of 1972; this one is in the guise of a VX 4/90, in pre-production (un-road-taxed) form secretly photographed at Vauxhall's own test ground at Millbrook. The other fronts belonged to sister cars, the six-pot Ventora and four-cylinder Victor models. The Ventora shared a similar harmonica grille to the one shown, except that a large Vauxhall griffin proudly mounted centrally replaced the white star on this VX 4/90. This Mark 1 "pre-spoiler" four-speed model could top 105 mph, yet still attain 30 mpg on a steady run — somewhat better than its immediate predecessor, the FD. The headlamps remained in pairs, as on its predecessor, although like the new Ventora's they were now square instead of round. Note the Ventora wheels on this pre-production car.

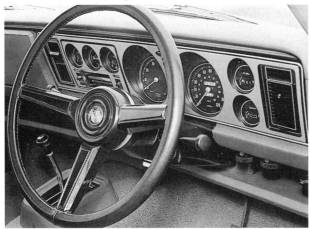

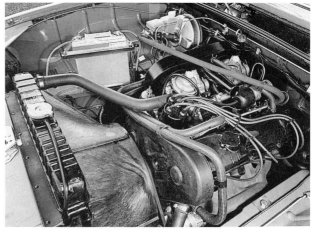

Above left: Photographed in late 1971, with 2207 miles already on the clock, this pilot-build VX 4/90 had the rare, almost unheard-of, optional automatic three-speed transmission. The facia layout was impressive, with a large, clear speedometer and rev counter deeply recessed at an angle (perhaps like the Cortina Mark 3 before its facelift?) to avoid reflections. The five smaller supplementary dials were replaced by just four in 1974. The temperature gauge to the right was moved far left and replaced the battery gauge; and in its old position came the switch for the headlamps, interior lamps, and panel lights. The steering wheel was substituted by a more modern design similar to the Magnum's. Wood panelling, an important feature in quality performance cars of the past, never appeared in the FE VX 4/90's interior. *Above right:* Twin carbs were the order of the day on this February 1972 shot — an early production FE VX 4/90. The slant four in 2279 cc form was basically a revamp of the earlier 2-litre unit. Note that this car is in rare automatic form (an auto fluid dipstick pipe is visible at the centre of the bulkhead).

Above left: One of the last "Phase 1" (for the want of a better name) VX 4/90s to be built. The registration plate indicates to the author that it was probably registered in October 1975, just a couple of months before production ran out. The VX 4/90 disappeared for 19 months, only to return in a more refreshing guise for a short 11-month production run. Compare this picture to earlier VX 4/90s shown elsewhere, and note the extra chrome embellishments around the wheel arches, and blackened wiper blades. Not visible here is a slightly revised dash layout. Above right: The interesting Phase 2 VX 490 FE (note lack of stroke in the designation), very few of which were reputed to have been made. Photographic evidence exists in the Vauxhall archives of a top line VX 490E model (an injected slant four 2300 model!), although this version was never marketed. Eighteen months elapsed between the earlier FE model (a four-speeder) and this (a five-speeder). Less than 1000 were manufactured; production ground to a halt at the same time as with the VX 1800 and 2300 FE models in summer 1978. The model shown must be an early prototype (as its British "R" registration letter also implies), as the spotlights, normally fitted beneath the bumper, are not fitted to this car. It has the 2300 GLS side/indicator lamps fitted (no doubt to plug the holes), making a total of three front indicators per side! New features included chrome wheel trims, a front air dam that added 12 mph to the top speed, different grille treatment and interior appointments. More importantly, the Phase 2 utilized the Getrag 5-speed gearbox, also seen in the 2300 HS Chevette.

Model	VX 4/90 FE
Dates of Production	March 1972 to January 1976; then August 1977 to summer 1978
Body Types	4-door saloon
Engines Offered	2279 cc (110 bhp, 1972-3; 116 bhp, 1974-5; then 118 bhp, 1977-8)
Transmission	4-speed manual; optional 3-speed automatic; then Getrag 5-speed manual on 1977-8 model only
Average Fuel Consumption	17 mpg (urban)
Mpg at 56 mph	32.8 mpg
Top Speed	105 mph
0-60 Mph	11.1 sec
Braking System	Dual circuit, servo-assisted, front disc, rear drums
Wheels and Tyres	Wheels: (1978) Sports 14; tyres: (1978) 185SR x 14
Dimensions	Length: 14 ft $10\frac{4}{5}$ in, width: 5 ft $6\frac{9}{10}$ in; height: 4 ft $5\frac{9}{10}$ in
Weight	2745 lb
Production Changes	Phase 2 included: addition of front spoiler, indicators moved to headlamps, chrome wheel trims, tartan trim
Price at Launch	£1524
Made at	Luton
Number Produced	18,042 (1972-6) 900 approx. (1977-8)

The completely revised interior of the much reworked VX 490 II. This was to be the last VX 490 offering after 15 years. The emphasis was always the same a sporty four-door family saloon based on the company's current mid-range family car. The tartan trim was similar to that used in HC Sportshatch models (all 197 of them!) and of course the 2300 HS Chevette. While the VX 1800 and 2300s offered wood veneer dash treatment, the VX 490 was equipped with a plain black/grey dash, but more detailed instrumentation. Twin carburettors boosted the 2300's bhp from 108 to 116 and an oil cooler was fitted as standard. For a while, at least until the arrival of the "hot hatch" GTE Astra of the early 1980s, Vauxhall was without a "special" sports car, for even the booted coupé derivative of the Cavalier (Manta lookalike) was discontinued in the late 1970s.

Model	Engine	From	To
VX4/90			
VX four ninety* FB	1507	2/62	7/63
VX 4/90 FB	1594	7/63	10/64
VX 4/90 FC	1594	10/64	9/67
VX 4/90 FD	1975	10/69	2/72
VX 4/90 (4-speed) FE	2279	3/72	1/76
VX 490 (5-speed) FE	2279	8/77	Summer 78

* Vauxhall changed the style of this designation over the years

6

The Viva
— The Baby
that Grew Up

In September 1963 the announcement was made that Vauxhall was to return to the 1-litre economy market with an entirely new two-door saloon called the Viva. This new car had been rumoured for some time, and was initially available in standard and de luxe forms. It was not too long before Vauxhall was enjoying another sales success, just as it had with the little Ten (as mentioned earlier, production of this sandwiched the Second World War). The new vehicle sold exceptionally well both on the home market and abroad: Canada, Australia and France, where it was named the Epic, and seemingly took a lot of orders.

The Viva design was simplicity itself. The Vauxhall styling shop had started with a clean sheet of paper. There were to be no American style influences on this vehicle based on a conventional three-box design. True, it did resemble the Opel Kadett, which had been available in Britain for 12 months by then. The chassis had very similar dimensions to the Opel and the wholly new 1057 cc cast-iron engine shared the same stroke, but with a slightly larger bore.

The de luxe model could be easily distinguished from its more basic sisters by its aluminium trim strips along its body flanks, and there were also three extra colours to choose from. The SL model joined the range in mid-1965 (SL stood for Super Luxury), and a "hot" SL90 was the final addition in September of that year. The Bedford Beagle estate car was another conversion, this time based on the 8 cwt — 900 lb to North Americans — van (this is described in Chapter 13). In December 1965 the 250,000th Viva rolled off the production line and, by the end of its run, 309,538 had been manufactured.

By the time of the 1966 London Motor Show, the HB Viva had arrived. Even though the HA had proved to be a rather successful seller, the HB models did even better. In four years, well over half a million were sold worldwide. The HBs introduced to Vauxhall more angular styling, and inherited the body swage just below the rear side windows from bigger-engined PC models — hence the name "Coke bottle" Viva. They came in many guises: the captions to the accompanying pictures speak for themselves. There were two-door versions, then an estate, a four-door and, of course the rare GT (*see* Chapter 12); with the many trim options there were altogether 26 different Vivas by the end of its production run! Apart from the 2-litre slant four GT, there were just two engine types: the 1159 cc and optional 1600 cc (and both could come with optional automatic transmission); and the 1159 cc could be ordered as a faster "90", which the Brabham Viva conversion was based on. Another conversion was the Crayford drophead based on any two-door version of the day, and very attractive it was. In Australia the HB Viva was marketed as the Holden Torana and lasted until 1969. It was then replaced by a much larger, all-Australian Torana, enjoying the benefits of a 2.85-litre six with triple Stromberg carburettors, in its more powerful GTR guise. This "LC" model shared the windscreen and door assemblies of the HB Viva. The Australian police were quick to realize the car's potential and switched from their Morris and Austin Mini Cooper S vehicles. Also available in 1300 cc form, the six-cylinder cars were given a longer nose. The car lasted until 1974, when it was replaced by the LH Torana.

The Viva HC enjoyed a production run more than twice as long as either of its HA or HB predecessors, and in its nine years offered more combinations of trim, body types and options than any other Vauxhall up to that time.

Perhaps the most popular style offered was the two-door saloon. Although it looked much larger than its immediate predecessor (no doubt due to the much larger glass area) it was only some 2 in wider and 1 in longer. Other body types included: a four-door saloon, based on the same wheelbase, but with shorter front doors; an estate fastback three-door — combining sporty looks with practicality; and a coupé (1976 only), the first of the economy E models. This last version was offered to the public soon after the demise of the now desirable HP Firenza "droop snoot". This was in an effort to use up any surplus bodyshells left over from the droop snoot's incredibly low production run. It was true that the Magnum was also offered with this body style, but it would seem that a very small number of these were built (just 5 per cent of total production). No van type based on the HC Viva was ever offered, although corporates such as DER television rental would blank out the rear-side windows to create a pseudo-van.

This time, Vauxhall chose to launch the new model at the Paris Motor Show.

Production of Vivas spanned the years 1963 to 1979. In all 309,538 HA Vivas were produced, 556,752 HBs and over 612,000 HCs. Strangely, production of the little HA Viva van even outlasted that of the HC. This popular small commercial vehicle was manufactured until well in to the early 1980s, selling mostly to the big corporates such as the Gas Board, British Rail, or the various regional Electricity Boards. The HA Viva was the only Viva available with just two doors although the Bedford Beagle, a more spacious factory-approved conversion by the Martin Walter group, was offered in the 1960s with twin opening rear doors based on the 8 cwt van version. The Dormobile Roma was also marketed, this, too, based on the little HA van concept. The British road tax discs on these vehicles date the picture to spring 1971, when it was taken by the marketing department celebrating the millionth Viva built on 20 July that year.

This was the second year running that new models had been announced here (the late arriving VX 4/90 had made its début in Paris in 1969). Available from October 1970, all production examples would have carried the British "J" registration mark, although some early proving photographs show HCs with H suffixes. As with the HB, the first of these Vivas were either 1159 cc powered, or had the optional 1599 cc unit. These engines were soon dropped (as early in fact as 1971 and 1972 respectively) and 1256 and 1759 cc engines were fitted. A 2279 cc unit (basically the same 2.3-litre slant four as used in the Victor, VX 4/90, Firenza and Magnum) was also available in tandem with the 1800.

Interestingly, although there was no replacement for the 2-litre HB GT in

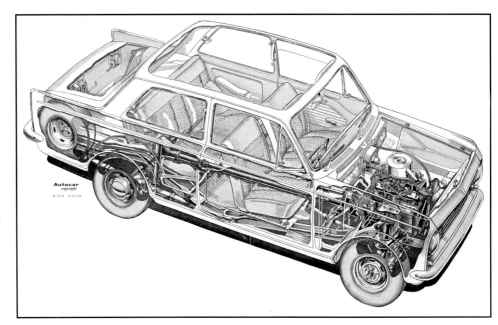

October 1963 brought the Viva HA, a modest two-door small family saloon, coil sprung at the front, and leaf at the rear. The advertisements stated that the "paint would never need polishing" thanks to the acrylic finish of the paintwork. All the HAs, the Standard, De Luxe (shown), SL and SL90 (both of 1965) were powered by a new ultra-small (certainly for contemporary Vauxhall cars) 1063 cc four-cylinder engine, with ratios of either 8.51, or an optional 7.31 for certain markets. This engine soon proved that small meant economy on the 1965 Mobil Economy event, an HA scored 44.11 mpg for the 1000-mile run.

Model	Viva HA
Dates of Production	September 1963 to September 1966
Body Types	2-door saloon, plus Bedford HA enclosed van, and Bedford Beagle
Engines Offered	1057 cc (50 bhp or 54 bhp on 90 version
Transmission	4-speed manual
Average Fuel Consumption	32 mpg; 28 mpg (SL 90); 28 mpg (Bedford Beagle)
Mpg at 56 mph	40 mpg; 38 mpg (SL 90); 33 mpg (Bedford Beagle)
Top Speed	80 mph; 70 mph (1159 cc: Bedford Beagle)
Braking System	Standard: drum brakes all round; SL 90: same but front disc
Wheels and Tyres	Wheels: 3.50B x 12L; tyres: 5.50 x 12 4 ply
Dimensions	Length: 12 ft $11\frac{1}{10}$ in; width: 4 ft $11\frac{2}{5}$ in; height: 4 ft $5\frac{3}{10}$ in
Weight	1564 lb (Standard); 1575 lb (De Luxe); 1680 lb (Bedford Beagle)
Production Changes	June 1964; minor changes to carburettors, timing chain lubricator, wax capsule type thermostat fitted, modified windscreen surround; September 1964: new indicator/light switch, steering gear raised by 20 per cent, choke control location modified, door trim, front seats on De Luxe, sound insulation, boot mat; November 1964; modifications to: oil filter, rear engine mounting, rear axle torque arm mounting, thicker gear lever
Price at Launch	£528 (base model) £566 (De Luxe)
Made at	Ellesmere Port (from 1 June 1964)
Number Produced	309,538 (Viva) 11,794 (HA 90)

this series, several full-scale fibreglass models were constructed on the HC theme, with an obvious sports design in mind. The "VXGT" was one of these mock-ups. With presumably false registration plates (VXE 396H), the model was in the coupé style with sports wheels, one-piece wrap-around rear light cluster unit, bumper overriders and twin rectangular exhaust outlets beneath the rear registration plate. From the front, it was obvious the designers had torn a page out of the VX 4/90 and Ventora FE model design book. Another mock-up, probably conceived shortly before the VXGT, was code-named HCR 1970. With the same rear lamp and exhaust outlet treatment, this prototype carried the HB GT's bonnet scoops (although slightly larger than before). The styling was not quite as the finished coupé would be (first introduced as the Firenza in

1971). For example, it had recessed doorhandles, similar to those on post-1971 Volvos, and different side window arrangements. Patient customers were to see why there was no GT replacement; a new Firenza model based loosely on these designs would be launched in 1971.

Although no official HC conversions existed, there were a couple of limited edition specials, namely the Viva Gold Riband, and the orange X14, the latter in either two- or four-door form, equipped with attractive Rostyle wheels and wider tyres and the option of an automatic 1759 cc engine. This was unusual since, except for the Ventora VIP, Vauxhall produced little in the way of limited editions until the early 1980s, when it seemed that all models were likely to give rise to some kind of special at any given time, as can be deduced from the comprehensive model listings set out in each chapter.

Very little changed in the HC's production run that is not covered in the accompanying photo captions. SLs and standard models became obsolete and were replaced by more modern-sounding Ls and GLSs, and the Magnum/Firenza seven dial dash was later used in the 1300GLS and 1800GLS Vivas (the 1800 took over from the Magnum, when this was finished in 1978). The last Viva rolled off the Ellesmere Port line in 1979, following in the tracks of over 612,000 of its kind. This was to be the end of the Viva — the baby that grew up into a medium-sized family saloon.

A contemporary press photograph displaying the tight turning circle of the then new HA in 1963. The caption read "A photographer's illustration of the turning circle that makes the Viva highly manoeuvrable in traffic and easy to park in confined spaces. The rack and pinion steering is light, and entirely free from road wheel vibration." The turning circle? A commendable 29 ft.

The "Coke bottle" HB replaced the smaller "Biscuit tin" HA on 21 September 1966. Its more contemporary styling brought instant success — half a million sold in four years of production proved this. To begin with, the only body style available was the two-door saloon. The car displayed on the left is the SL, and on the right is the De Luxe. Both of these housed the new 1159 cc power train in either standard (47 bhp), or uprated 90 (69 bhp) form. Automatics, estates, four-doors, the 1600 cc option and GTs came later.

Model	Viva HB
Dates of Production	September 1966 to August 1970
Body Types	2-door saloon; 4-door saloon; 3-door estate
Engines Offered	1159 cc (47 bhp, 56 bhp or – 90-69 bhp); 1599 cc (83 bhp); 1975 cc (112 bhp)
Transmission	4-speed manual; optional GM 3-speed automatic
Average Fuel Consumption	25 mpg
Mpg at 56 mph	32.5 mpg
Top Speed	75-85 mph (GT 104 mph)
0–60 Mph	19.7 sec (Viva 1159) 11.4 sec (Viva GT)
Braking System	De Luxe and SL: drums front and rear; 90 models: servo with front disc, rear drums
Wheels and Tyres	Wheels: pressed steel $3\frac{1}{2}$B x 12 (De Luxe), 4J x 12 (90 and 1600 models), $4\frac{1}{2}$ x 13 (GT); tyres: 5.50 x 12 (De Luxe and SL), 6.2 x 12 (1600 and 90), 165/70 HR x 13 low profile (GT)
Dimensions	Length: 13 ft 5 in; width: 5 ft 3 in; height: 4 ft $5\frac{1}{4}$ in
Weight	2-door: 1704 lb (Standard); 1955 lb (1600 De Luxe); 4-door: 1780 lb (De Luxe); Estate: 1878 lb (De Luxe)
Production Changes	Automatic available from February 1967; estate from June 1967; 2-litre GT from March 1968; option of 1600 cc engine from June 1968
Price at Launch	£579 (Basic); £626 (De Luxe); £672 (SL); £663 (De Luxe 90); £708 (SL 90); £1062 12s 10d (GT)
Made at	Saloons: Ellesmere Port GTs and estates: Luton
Number Produced	556,391 (HB) 78,296 (HB 90) 13,517 (1600) 4,606 (GT)

There was 43.5 cu ft of load space available in the HB estate series. These models were introduced in June 1967, which was 9 months after the HB arrived on the scene and 15 months before the four-door. Like Ford's Escort, the estate came as a three-door only, and allowed loads of up to 5 ft in length to be carried. Prices started at £729 in Standard trim.

The HB Viva estate was offered in either 1159 cc or 1599 cc form and was quite an attractive load carrier in its day. This is the De Luxe. A more up-market SL and livelier SL90 were also sold, complete with more ornate wheel trims, and a coachline that followed that distinctive curve of the side glass, shown clearly here hence the nickname of "Coke bottle". Note that the saloon's loading sill was retained, which allowed use of the same rear lamp clusters, and the same location of the fuel filler cap. A successful car the HB Viva was at its peak it took 11 per cent of home sales, and there were up to 26 models to choose from.

This seemingly anonymous car, in left-hand-drive export form, would have sported a British "G" suffix had it been registered. The four-door HB became available from October 1968, some 24 months into production. The four-door treatment looked something of an afterthought (although arguably not nearly as bad as the four-door derivative of the Mark 1 Escort). The new four-door choice added eight new models to a line-up that now totalled 26. The trusty 1159 cc (in standard or "90" form) and optional 83 bhp 1599 cc engines powered the new models, but Viva GTs and estate versions were not offered in this form. HB Vivas such as the one pictured here were exported via Newport Docks, and demand was so heavy at one point that Vauxhall had to charter its own ship!

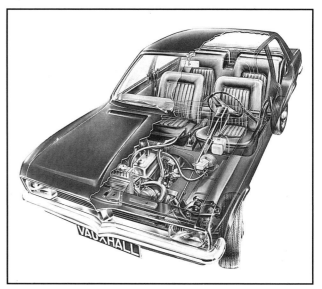

Perhaps one of the earliest HC Vivas built, BXE 227H (registered in July 1970, but other photos show another early untaxed Viva NMB 405H), on trial at the relatively new Vauxhall proving ground at Millbrook. No doubt this particular car had travelled thousands of punishing miles on rough surfaces, through water, dust tunnels, around high speed circuits and up and down steep hills. We may wonder if this early example ever survived and was sold off; or perhaps it was driven into a brick wall for the mandatory safety testing. The HC Viva was truly the last Vauxhall designed without evidence of Opel connections. The FE series of March 1972 shared the same floorpan as its German Opel cousins; and the 1975 Chevette was part of General Motors' worldwide T Car concept.

Model	Viva HC
Dates of Production	October 1970 to June 1979
Body Types	2-door saloon; 2 door-coupé; 4-door saloon; 3-door estate
Engines Offered	1159 cc (49 bhp, 59 bhp or -90-72 bhp); 1256 cc (62.5 bhp); 1599 cc (80 bhp); 1759 cc (88 bhp); 2279 cc (110 bhp)
Transmission	4-speed manual; 3-speed automatic
Average Fuel Consumption	33 mpg (1159 cc saloon); 32 mpg (1256 cc saloon); 21 mpg (1800 saloon); 19 mpg (1800 saloon automatic)
Mpg at 56 mph	38 mpg (1159 cc); 40 mpg (1256 cc); 35 mpg (1800 cc); 30 mpg (1800 automatic)
Top Speed	79 mph (1159 cc); 86 mph (1256 cc)
0-60 Mph	18.1 sec (1256 cc) 11.5 sec (2300 cc)
Braking System	Servo-assisted, front disc, rear drums; heavy duty with larger-engined Vivas
Wheels and Tyres	Wheels: Viva E, Standard, and L: $4\frac{1}{2}$ in steel; GLS: 5 in sports wheels; tyres: Viva E: 5.60 x 13 cross-ply (radial optional); Standard, L and GLS: 155SR x 13 radials
Dimensions	Length: 13 ft 6 in, width: 5 ft 5 in, height: 4 ft $5\frac{1}{10}$ in
Weight	1903 lb (1159 cc 4-door); 1837 lb (1256 cc 2-door)
Production Changes	Engine enlarged from 1159 cc to 1256 cc, 1972; and 1599 cc option upgraded to 1759 cc; many trim changes throughout its history
Price at Launch	£783
Made at	Mainly at Ellesmere, but 20% at Luton
Number Produced	549,288 (saloons) 91,575 (estates)

Above left: *It took three years and over £3.5 million to transform the previously barren landscape at Millbrook into what is now recognized as one of Europe's most modern proving grounds. One part of the 700-acre site in Bedfordshire allows room here for 20 ex-test cars awaiting further disposal. The Vivas shown are left-hand-drive Canadian market models badged (interestingly) as Pontiac Firenzas, with mandatory laminated front screens. Note, too, the FE estate and FD saloons, probably dating this picture to about 1972. Among Millbrook's extensive facilities are a 2-mile, five-lane circular motorway, 1.5 miles of country roads, hill routes (up to 1 in 4), fresh- and saltwater-splashes, a dust tunnel, Belgian-style pavé courses, and an outdoor impact barrier.*

Above right: *An early interior photograph of the Viva SL (SL stood for Super Luxury) fitted with optional automatic transmission. Although very spartan by today's standards, the brochures said of the car "This is the car to revel in. Deep pile carpets, wall to wall, rich upholstery throughout — right up to window level. A centre console housing a smartly gaitered gearshift, with a built-in ashtray. We won't let you forget what luxury is for a moment."*

Top of the range Viva, the four-door Viva SL of 1971. Earliest HCs were powered by the four-cylinder 1159 cc (ex-HB) unit, or optional 1599 cc (ex- HB and FD) slant four. In August 1971, less than a year into production, the introduction of the slightly more powerful 1256 cc engine (a successful engine that lasted some 13 years until the disappearance of the Chevette) brought the departure of the 1159. A short while later, (in March 1972) the optional 1599 was replaced by either the 1759 cc or 2279 cc slant four (depending on customer engine choice) as used in the new FE range. Note here the whitewall tyres used on this British specification SL press car, along with optional mirrors, foglamps, radio aerial, and vinyl-covered roof.

Above left: A Blydenstein-tuned 2-litre Firenza on the Millbrook test track with fifth wheel attached (not shown), in the summer of 1971. Although the exact extra power is not known to the author, no doubt a few hundred squashed flies would testify to the car's high performance! Within a year the 2-litre slant four had gone replaced by the 2.3-litre slant four. *Above right:* The sight of British cars of any make brought together for mass export is always heart-warming to the true patriot, and this view is no exception. Among MG Midgets and Hillman Avengers, this consignment of 836 Vivas was bound for Canada. Badged as Firenzas, these cars were caught by the camera at Newport Docks early in 1971. Note the large number of official export stickers on the vehicles' windows, the mandatory twin front headlamp treatment, lack of hub caps (standard shipping practice) and occasional whitewall tyres. All models are fitted with the side repeater lamps specifically for Canada. By July 1971, these exports had helped the millionth Viva roll off the production line.

An early morning photograph before the mad rush at the 1972 Motor Show. These shows often feature new models, or new trim or often limited edition versions of existing models; the Viva X14 and Viva Gold Riband of 1972 are good examples. The numberplate of the revolving Viva SL typifies 1970s marketing "It's a joy to drive".

The most potent of all standard production Vivas was manufactured for just 18 months in the 1972–3 season. The 2279 cc slant four Viva SL saloon and estates came equipped with Rostyle wheels, seven-dial instrument binnacle (later adopted by the HP Firenza and 2.3-litre Magnums and, ultimately, the Viva 1300 GLS), reversing lamps and side stripes. It could top around 100 mph, and accelerate 0–60 mph in just 11.5 seconds (12.5 for the estate), all for a British price of £1218 (saloon) or £1306 (estate). These versions were dropped in favour of the new Magnum (originally marketed for a while as the Viva Magnum) in September 1973. The estate version shown here was dubbed "the poor man's Scimitar GTE", and like the saloon could only be identified as a large-engined Viva from a modest badge mounted on the grille. Bill Blydenstein marketed the Viva Ecosse via the SMT group in Scotland, based on the 2300 estate and identified by extra driving lamps and oversize tyres. Among detail improvements there were quartz halogen headlamps, hazard flashers, inertia reel belts, map and under-bonnet lamps, a dipping rear view mirror, four mudflaps, anti-lift wiper blades, a first aid kit, a fire extinguisher and electric washers in fact everything appealing to the sporty long-distance driver. A creditable 110 mph top speed was thanks to a Stage III engine with a modified head.

The history of the cheapest Vauxhall available in late 1975 is an interesting one. Faced with a large number of new unused bodyshells from the discontinued High Performance Firenza (the "droop snoot") and the coupé derivative of the Magnum (which had proved to be unpopular), the marketing men came up with the ingenious solution of building a base model named Viva E (E for economy in this case), powered by the standard 1256 cc power unit. With black trim, and no frills attached (although advertisements were proud to boast a handbrake warning lamp!), the limited production E became a popular economy car. Indeed Vauxhall soon saw fit to introduce E versions of both two- and four-door Viva saloons (and a year later to the Chevette range), which lasted until 1979. Normally, the numberplates of British-registered E coupés had the newest letter available for this bodyshell, namely "P". The body was styled by David Jones, Vauxhall's head of styling, and had first appeared on the original Firenza of 1971. The E coupé, available in the colours Monaco white or optional bronze gold starfire or blue fire, sold for £1399, amazingly £283 cheaper than the new standard Chevette, and £133 cheaper than the basic Viva, so its popularity was easily understood.

Model	Engine	From	To
HA			
Viva	1057	9/63	9/66
Viva De Luxe	1057	9/63	9/66
Bedford Beagle	1057	10/64	–
Viva SL	1057	6/65	9/66
Viva SL90	1057	late 65	9/66
HB			
Viva saloon 2-door (fleet only)	1159	9/66	9/70
Viva De Luxe saloon 2-door	1159	9/66	9/70
Viva 90 De Luxe saloon 2-door	1159	9/66	9/70
Viva saloon SL 2-door	1159	9/66	9/70
Viva saloon 90 SL 2-door	1159	9/66	9/70
Viva De Luxe estate	1159	6/67	9/70
Viva 90 De Luxe estate	1159	6/67	9/70
Viva estate SL	1159	6/67	9/70
Viva estate SL 90	1159	6/67	9/70
Viva GT (Mark 1)	1975	3/68	7/69
Viva 1600 De Luxe saloon 2-door	1599	6/68	9/70
Viva 1600 SL saloon 2-door	1599	6/68	9/70
Viva De Luxe 1600 estate	1599	6/68	9/70
Viva SL 1600 estate	1599	6/68	9/70
Viva De Luxe saloon 4-door	1159	9/68	9/70
Viva 90 De Luxe saloon 4-door	1159	9/68	9/70
Viva SL saloon 4-door	1159	9/68	9/70
Viva SL90 saloon 4-door	1159	9/68	9/70
Viva GT (Mark 2)	1975	8/69	9/70
Brabham Viva (on "90" models)	1159	9/66	1968
Crayford (convertible)	Any	9/66	9/70
HC			
Viva 2-door	1159	10/70	7/71
Viva De Luxe 2-door	1159	10/70	7/71
Viva De Luxe 4-door	1159	10/70	7/71
Viva De Luxe estate 3-door	1159	10/70	7/71
Viva De Luxe 90 2-door	1159	10/70	7/71
Viva De Luxe 90 4-door	1159	10/70	7/71
Viva De Luxe 90 estate 3-door	1159	10/70	7/71
Viva De Luxe SL90 2-door	1159	10/70	7/71
Viva De Luxe SL90 4-door	1159	10/70	7/71
Viva De Luxe SL90 estate 3-door	1159	10/70	7/71
Viva SL 1600 2-door	1599	10/70	12/71
Viva SL 1600 4-door	1599	10/70	12/71
Viva SL 1600 estate 3-door	1599	10/70	3/72
Viva Standard 2-door	1256	8/71	12/73
Viva De Luxe 2-door	1256	8/71	10/75
Viva De Luxe 4-door	1256	8/71	10/75
Viva De Luxe estate 3-door	1256	8/71	10/75
Viva SL 2-door	1256	8/71	10/75

Viva SL 4-door	1256	8/71	10/75
Viva SL estate 3-door	1256	8/71	10/75
Viva Gold Riband 2-door Limited Edition	1256	10/71	–
Viva X14 2-door Limited Edition	1256	1972	–
Viva X14 4-door Limited Edition	1256	1972	–
Viva X14 2-door Limited Edition	1759	1972	–
Viva X14 4-door Limited Edition	1759	1972	–
Viva SL 1800 2-door	1759	3/72	10/75
Viva SL 1800 4-door	1759	3/72	10/75
Viva SL 1800 estate 3-door	1759	3/72	10/75
Viva SL 2300 2-door	2279	3/72	9/73
Viva SL 2300 4-door	2279	3/72	9/73
Viva SL 2300 estate 3-door	2279	3/72	9/73
Viva DS (Driving School Spec.)	1256	6/74	–
Viva S57 saloon	1256	3/74	–
Viva S 2-door Limited Edition	1256	2/75	–
Viva S saloon 4-door Limited Edition	1256	2/75	–
Viva 1300 2-door	1256	10/75	1976
Viva 1300 4-door	1256	10/75	1976
Viva 1300 estate 3-door	1256	10/75	1976
Viva 1300L 2-door	1256	10/75	6/79
Viva 1300L 4-door	1256	10/75	6/79
Viva 1300L estate 3-door	1256	10/75	6/79
Viva 1300SL 2-door	1256	10/75	11/76
Viva 1300SL 4-door	1256	10/75	11/76
Viva 1300SL estate 3-door	1256	10/75	11/76
Viva 1800L 2-door	1759	10/75	4/78
Viva 1800L 4-door	1759	10/75	4/78
Viva 1800L estate 3-door	1759	10/75	4/78
Viva 1800SL automatic 2-door	1759	10/75	11/76
Viva 1800SL automatic 4-door	1759	10/75	11/76
Viva 1800SL estate automatic 3-door	1759	10/75	11/76
Viva E 2-door	1256	10/75	6/79
Viva E 4-door	1256	10/75	6/79
Viva E coupé 2-door	1256	10/75	1976
Viva 1300GLS 2-door	1256	11/76	6/79
Viva 1300GLS 4-door	1256	11/76	6/79
Viva 1300GLS estate 3-door	1256	11/76	6/79
Viva 1800GLS 4-door	1759	4/78	6/79

7

Chevettes and Novas — From Hatches to Saloons

The Chevette, launched primarily as a trend-setting three-door hatchback in March 1975, was the first of a string of new Vauxhalls that were originally Opel-based. The new car, advertised widely on television and in the contemporary press as "whatever you want it to be", was actually a derivation of the American giant's T car, which had appeared a year and a half earlier. The T car project was similar to that of the later J car (the Vauxhall Mark 2 Cavalier) and V car (Carlton, Royale, etc.) in that it was a basic design that could be tailored to suit a country's specific requirements in trim, transmission and power format, whether for local taste or legal reasons. The small T car first appeared in Brazil, and was subsequently produced in West Germany (Opel), Japan (Isuzi), Britain (Vauxhall), Argentina (Chevrolet) and the United States (Chevrolet and Pontiac).

It was no secret that the Chevette's nearest cousins were the German-built 993 cc and 1196 cc Opel Kadetts. This 1973 model was available in a wider variety of guises than the Chevette (particularly at the start of the latter's production run, as initially it only appeared as a three-door hatchback). For as well as two- and four-door saloons, three-door hatchbacks (a later model called the Opel Kadett City), and three-door estate versions, there was also a Kadett two-door fastback sports coupé. However, neither Opel nor Vauxhall produced a five-door estate version. The fastback bodystyle was also offered in the form of the Japanese-built T car, the Isuzi Gemini, a peculiar combination of British-type bodywork with Japanese trim and running components; its 1600 cc engine and transmission were Japanese. Just to add to the confusion, the Isuzi Gemini was marketed in the United States as an Opel! Chevrolet launched its Chevette in America in early 1976 and quite rightly claimed it to be the most economic new car on that market. In contrast to the monstrous gas-guzzlers available in the United States at that time, the Chevrolet Chevette Scooter, as it was known in its most basic form, could return 40 mpg — quite remarkable as far as American cars go. Although ugly (at least to European eyes), with bulbous trim and ghastly whitewall tyres, the Americans enjoyed economical motoring with brisk performance and reasonable ride comfort. However, one American magazine tester complained that unfortunately you had to sit on the seats and not in them! Surprisingly, the Chevrolet Chevette was also offered as a four-door on the same wheelbase, but Europeans had to look twice, through all that seemingly alien trim, to discover the familiar Chevette underneath.

Australia also shared the T car: the Holden Gemini appeared in March 1975 basically resembling our own Chevette. A van version was also offered.

Back in Britain, the new Chevette was received with some amazement from the motoring public: it was the first true British-built hatchback. Cars such as the Renault 5, very successful in Europe and dating from 1972, and the larger Renault 16 had already proved the popularity of a rear door. Ford's "Bobcat" project — the Fiesta — was not to arrive until the following year, and the front-wheel-drive Metro, of course, not for half a decade. The Maxi of 1969 did have a rear hatch, but was a little too large to be put in the true

All is not what it seems this was the first production Chevette, made on 10 February 1975. However, this model followed 16 prototypes tried and tested overseas in deserts, on mountain ranges, in snow and slush, and also at the company's own proving ground at Milbrook, where over a million gruelling miles were covered, punishing the Chevettes over every type of surface. Between the prototypes and the model shown here were a handful of pre-production cars built to check the smoothness of the assembly line, and to give the press something to road-test for publication on D day!

The mid-1970s brought the Chevette, a car claimed by Vauxhall as "Whatever you want it to be". The early 15-minute dealer promotional film featured Rodney Bewes, of the TV Likely Lads *series, suitably dressed in flared trousers and platform shoes. A much shorter TV advertisement with similar music praised the Chevette as three cars a handy estate, a sporty coupé, and a family saloon. Here, a 1975 Chevette L — top model for the day — poses for the camera among the daffodils.*

Model	Chevette (T car)
Dates of Production	March 1975 to March 1984
Body Types	3-door hatchback; 2-door saloon; 4-door saloon; 3-door estate; van
Engines Offered	All 1256 cc (58.5 bhp) except 2300 HS/HSR 2297 cc (135 bhp)
Transmission	4-speed manual; 2300HS/HSR 5-speed manual
Average Fuel Consumption	31 mpg (1256 cc); 17.4 mpg (2300 HSR)
Mpg at 56 mph	45 mpg (1256 cc); 34.4 mpg (2300HS/HSR)
Top Speed	91 mph (1256 cc); over 115 mph (2300HS/HSR)
0-60 Mph	14.5 sec (1256 cc); 8.5 sec (2300 HS)
Braking System	Servo-assisted, front disc, rear drums
Wheels and Tyres	Wheels: steel, 5 in rims (except HS); tyres: 155SR x 13 on all models except GLS: 175 x 13; 2300HS/HSR 205/60HR x 13
Dimensions	Length: 12 ft 11$\frac{7}{10}$ in (saloon); 11 ft 10 in (hatch); width: 5 ft 0$\frac{6}{10}$ in (saloon), 5 ft 0 in (hatch); height: 4 ft 5$\frac{1}{2}$ in (saloon), 4ft 5$\frac{7}{10}$ in (hatch)
Weight	1879 lb (hatchback); 2235 lb (2300HS)
Production Changes	Phase 2 from early 1980 (flush headlamps)
Price at Launch	£1649
Made at	Ellesmere Port
Number Produced	415,608
Also Available as	Opel Kadett, and 4-door 1.6-litre Chevrolet Chevette, Isuzu Gemini, Holden Gemini

Eighteen months after the launch, the last of the alternative body styles available for the Chevette was the three-door estate, which shared the extra length of the saloon vehicles. Soon came the Bedford Chevanne, basically a vehicle with the same layout as the estate, but without the side glass and rear seats, and competing with the HA Viva van.

hatchback category. Perhaps a little overlooked here (or possibly ahead of its time?), the Austin A40 of the early 1960s had a rear hatch in one version, but after this was dropped it was never replaced by a similar design.

After the March 1975 launch, the eager public had to wait seven weeks for production examples to become available. The flavour was certainly aimed at the sports/family area, with a bright range of eye-catching colours, available on either standard or L decor models. All models from day one boasted a two-speed fan, sports steering wheel, radial tyres, reclining front seats, and the trusty 58 bhp 1256 cc Viva engine. The car could be hustled along at up to 90 mph, yet was still capable of over 40 mpg while touring.

It can be assumed that even at the March launch, Vauxhall had not yet come to a final decision on how many different trim variants of the Chevette there were to be. Thus the question of whether to have a basic version with some key equipment items deleted had not been settled by that spring of 1975, and several cosmetic changes to the range occurred in subsequent months. For example, October 1975 (during the United Kingdom "P" registration letter year) brought the first addition to the range, the Chevette GL. This had better trim, including a new centre console, and doors with carpeting and storage

Although a saloon version of the Chevette was not announced until mid-1976, the General Motors Corporation had been building cars on the T car theme for some time. Already on sale in Britain was the Opel Kadett saloon, which later became available as the Opel Kadett City a three-door hatch resembling a Chevette in all but name and front end treatment. The Opel lacked the Vauxhall's sloping nose, first featured in fact in Brazil in 1974 on the near-identical Chevrolet Chevette. The model shown is an L two-door.

A Chevette two-door saloon undergoes a quality control check at the company's Ellesmere Port plant, where all Chevettes were built. Note, in this carefully posed picture the stray VX 2300GLS behind (and the can of Three-in-One oil in the engineer's pocket!).

pockets, and brightwork, with sports road wheels with wider 175 radials, bumper overriders and so on. The rather spartan E version became available in January 1976, a base model aimed particularly at the fleet-buying sector of the market. This model was easily distinguishable externally from its up-market relatives: there was no bright strip on either the front or the rear screen, while plastic seats (described enthusiastically as Vynide in the brochures) were the order of the day inside. The following April, Vauxhall saw fit to rename all the model variants, thus the Standard became the L, the L became the GL, and a new GLS model replaced the GL. The E version remained unaffected.

The larger, more flush headlamps identify this as a "Phase 2" Chevette from 1980. The Chevette was a popular vehicle with the British armed forces the Ministry of Defence placed an order for 2000 of them in 1982. Chevettes are still popular on the second-hand market, a tribute to their combination of performance, reliability and economy.

Soon after these trim details had been sorted out both two- and four-door saloon body versions were launched, and so the public could finally see the full resemblance of the Chevette to the Opel Kadett family. The two-door (only available in E or L trim) shared its doors with the hatchback. Like many other two/four-door cars, however, the four-door version had shorter front doors. This model was available in E, L or GLS trim. An estate, only available in L décor with three doors, was available from September 1976.

Chevette production continued until the 1980s, when revised lamp clusters replaced the smaller units (these so easily filled with snow on winter

The American styling of the late 1950s influenced both the Victor and the Cresta/Velox models. This early Cresta reveals that influence abundantly, as excess chrome, a garish colour, and tailfins bear witness. Those tailfins got even more pronounced by the end of the decade, and even a chrome "V" motif was added to them — and a lot more chromework embellished the body, too. The specification of this Cresta dates the car to between August 1959 and August 1960; the later date coincided with the arrival of the larger 2651 cc six pot engine. Too much for some folk was the candy floss pink mono-tone coachwork option — some examples survive at the time of writing. The two millionth Vauxhall was a PA Cresta, made in February 1959.

October 1962 brought the PB range of Cresta and Velox vehicles with the now familiar 2651 cc straight-six power plant. By the 1964 Motor Show, a massive 25 per cent increase in the Cresta's capacity to 3293 cc produced 26 per cent more torque and 21 per cent more power, turning the luxury family saloon into a very fast vehicle for its day, out-accelerating, for example, the legendary Austin and Morris 1275S Coopers, the Porsche 1600C, the Lotus Cortina, and even the Rolls-Royce Silver Cloud. Almost lost in time is this October 1962 PB advertisement, well worth quoting "The big Vauxhall is not revolutionary, but is very nearly perfect. In twenty years it will be remembered, not for any one refinement, but for its masterful design, its completeness. It is quite simply a great motor car."

Martin Walter's PB estate conversion arrived in late 1963. The Folkestone firm was now recognized for this work and the Vauxhall company itself gave full warranty and approval to such models. Basing this kind of conversion job on such a large car meant that it was one of the most powerful load carriers of its time — even more so when the PB range's cubic capacity was raised by a tremendous 25 per cent a year or so later. The 3.71 axle ratio was a little low for the car to achieve a true 100 mph on the flat, but a highly respectable 0–60 mph time of 10.5 seconds (with the optional four-speed box) was truly remarkable, surprisingly at least 2 seconds quicker than the similarly weighted, but much more modern FE Ventora, which used the same engine a decade or so later.

Main picture: The Luton-produced Viscount of 1966 was an even more up-market Cresta. Standard equipment included power-assisted steering, electric windows (at least 10 years ahead of any other Vauxhall), and powerglide transmission. Like the Royale of the 1970s, and the Senator 2 of the late 1980s, in its year the Viscount was the most luxuriously appointed Vauxhall to date. In total 60,937 PCs were built between 1965 and 1972, and just 7025 of them were Viscounts — an average of about 20 per week. The vinyl-covered roof started a trend — many luxury vehicles from other companies were soon to copy this new idea, especially in the 1970s.

Inset: To how many readers will this bring back memories? The menacing view of a large police vehicle waiting outside the school gates in the late 1960s! This picture has been carefully chosen for two main reasons: firstly, it proves that all police cars were not either white, blue or black; secondly, most PC Crestas sold seemed to be of the de luxe variety; this car is not, as is shown by the now very rarely seen single headlamp treatment and correspondingly wider grille. Note the modest cross-ply tyres on this 140 bhp giant.

The crowning glory of the Viscount was the high level of equipment. The quality image was accentuated by a walnut veneer facia and wood inserts on the doors — essential to a British car that aspired to the "luxury" label. Power-operated windows — very advanced for the mid-1960s, were fitted to all the doors, and front seat occupants had inertia reel safety belts. Not visible here are the rear reading lamps and picnic tables built into the rear of the front seats. These front seats had Chapman Reuter hinges, allowing them to tilt right back to make a bed — as copied by the Austin Maxi in April 1969, and numerous cars since.

The 250,000th Victor was manufactured in December 1959 no single British vehicle had managed the quarter million mark in such a short space of time. The Victor was the first model produced in a new 1.5 million ft² assembly building at Luton, part of the £36 million expansion scheme. Some of the 50-odd models here in this late 1960 post-production line-up are shown in left-hand-drive form. Over 164,000 of the first quarter million were exported (86,000 to North America alone); thus the Victor was Britain's number one export vehicle. Series 2 Victors, as these models are, were quickly produced at the rate of 25,000 per week. When introduced, Vauxhall stated "The whole emphasis is on clean, smooth, purposeful lines. There is a new bonnet, new grille, new bumpers and side lamps. New rear wings and door panels, new boot lid, a new shape to the front of the roof."

Below: All body types except the six-cylinder models are depicted here in this late 1963 line-up. From left to right a calypso red Viva HA De Luxe, a facelifted Victor saloon, and a Victor estate. The vehicles are photographed at the entrance to 'Alameda de los Descalzos' in Lima, Peru. The press blurb stated "this area was used in Spanish colonial days by grandees and their ladies as an enclosed walk, a very popular recreation in the afternoons."

Above: Keen to exhibit an example of the new Victor estate at the Copenhagen show, Vauxhall brought forward the launch to 28 February 1958. The specification, it was announced, was virtually identical to its F type sister saloons, although a few well-thought-of enhancements had been made. These included an increase in rear axle ratio, heavier gauge axle tubes, an increase from three to five semi-elliptic rear springs and wider rear tyres. Vauxhall was proud of the new model — it was the company's first "shooting brake" produced totally in house. As the Vauxhall press office was quick to point out "It takes three seconds to fold away the rear seat, to give the extra load space, and both the wide tail door, and the two rear side doors can then be used for loading and unloading." The model shown dates from 1959, and is in popular two-tone horizon blue and white.

The 101 FC series offered more room, more comfort and greater refinement than its immediate predecessor, the FB. Available in four-door saloon, five-door estate and a faster, more distinctive VX 4/90 model, the FC introduced the revolutionary "space curve" look to Vauxhall. This ingenious new style not only added torsional strength to the bodywork — which in turn allowed more positive handling — but added vital extra inches to the interior without taking up more road space. Note this press vehicle has a door- (rather than wing-) mounted mirror, now of course commonplace on modern cars.

Prominent features of the FD Victor were its low waistline, and ultra-slim windscreen pillars. Obvious rivals in 1967 were the Ford Corsair, Hillman Hunter and Singer Vogue. Twin-headlamp treatment remained with all Victors, VX 4/90s and Ventoras, and the attractive style even continued into some FE models. However, the most significant change was the adoption of the slant four engine in 1.6- or 2-litre form, an over-head cam unit developed over the previous four years.

Above left: Although the FD Victors arrived in late 1967, it was not until late 1968 that Vauxhall announced that it had shoehorned the Cresta/Viscount 3294 cc engine under the bonnet and called the new model the Ventora. Dubbed the "Lazy Fireball", the new model was distinguished from its less powerful relatives by its attractive harmonica grille, its vinyl-covered roof (although this was optional originally), and additional chrome on the rear panel. There was soon to be press criticism of some of the car's shortcomings, and a much revamped Ventora II arrived in October 1969. This featured higher gearing, reclining seats (at last) and a better interior. Many of its previous options, reversing lamps for example, were made standard equipment. **Above right:** *A rev counter, wood-grained dash, horizontal slatted grille, and body side flash on these FBs meant one thing: VX four ninety (the designation was spelled out at this stage). Soon following the steps of the FB Victor, the VX four ninety (type FBH) came in ten colours in saloon form only. Then in 1964 another 2½ bhp was developed from an extra 86 cc and a corresponding increase in torque from the new 1594 cc engine, which had an aluminium cylinder head and a pair of Zenith carburettors.*

An idyllic Scottish landscape is the setting for this Yellow Gold 1973 Victor 1800 saloon. Available in both saloon (four-door only) and fastback estate versions, the model lasted until the summer of 1978 (although in the form of the VX 1800 from early 1976), when it was dropped in favour of the West German-design Carlton models. Power was not this vehicle's strong point the more economical Cortina 1600 could easily outpace the 1800 Victor in acceleration trials, and *have a slightly higher top speed. This model has the single reclinable front seats. The very earliest FE 1800 Victors still used the rather dated bench seat, in ambla trim.*

An original VX 4/90 FE dating back to spring 1972, photographed a month ahead of launch at Luton airport for the *Vauxhall Motorist* magazine. The engines fitted to VX 4/90s became larger and more sophisticated throughout the production run. This untaxed example has the 2279 cc slant four: the Phase 2 VX490 FE had the same basic engine but was much quicker, and had five gears. When the VX 1800 and 2300 models were killed off in summer 1978 the VX 490 went too, after a 16-year history.

After the departure of the Ten it took Vauxhall over a decade and a half to return to the small four-seater market, by introducing the original Viva, a small three-box design, reminiscent of Opel's Kadett. And how styling had changed since those pre-war days! Gone were those separate front wheel arches and headlamp units — and three cheers for the arrival of a sensible boot! This is the de luxe model nearly 310,000 were produced in its three-year production run. Many were exported, Canada taking many deliveries and rebadging them as Epic or Envoy (as did France), and in Australia the HA was particularly popular with the police.

Some countries took CKD (completely knocked down) Vauxhalls and assembled them on site. Places where this took place included Antwerp, for Belgium, Holland, Luxembourg and West Germany; Copenhagen, for Denmark; Bienne, for Switzerland; Melbourne, for Australia, New Guinea and the Solomon Islands; Wellington, for New Zealand; and Port Elizabeth, for South Africa.

These three Vivas represent 16 years of continuous Viva production of the car, with 1.5 million sold, both home and abroad. From left to right Viva HA De Luxe of 1963, Viva SL HB of 1966 (SL indicated by different grille treatment), and a 1971 Viva four-door SL. The last Viva came off the Ellesmere Port production line in December 1979. All Vivas, except the very first of the HAs, were produced here, from the time it opened for car manufacture in June 1964.

New wheels, trim and brightwork, and deeper more flush headlamps identify this as a second generation Chevette. Apart from the 400 or so "homologation special" 2300 HS/HSR models, all Chevettes had the 1256 cc power unit first offered in the HC Vivas and basic Firenza cars in 1971. The final 1256 cc engine was manufactured in 1984 and fitted to the last Chevette, completed on 28 March of that year. This Chevette four-door GL saloon in Carmine Red is seen in a splendid limestone setting of Gordale Scar, in the Yorkshire Dales.

Above left: New vehicles announced by Vauxhall in the late 1970s and early 1980s were basically rebadged Opels; the Vauxhall Nova, originally the Opel Corsa was manufactured in Spain, originally in two-door hatch form (shown here) or three-door saloon. Later came the five-door hatches and four-door saloons (but no estate version); the three-door hatch was the only derivative to retain those rather attractive boxed arches throughout. An appealing SR was quick to join the range, with 70 bhp and five speeds, and as late as 1988 there was the introduction of the superfast 1600 cc 16-valve fuel-injected GTE.

Above right: White Gold metallic is an unusual colour to see on a Carlton Mark 1, for it normally appears on the top Royale models. The 2-litre Carlton Mark 1 was part of the V car project, and shared many of its components with the Opel Commodore and Rekord models, except for Vauxhall's distinctive sloping nose. This is a Phase 2 Mark 1, built at Luton where this picture was taken, with more aerodynamic mirrors, revised wheels, a better Opel-style dash and revamped seat and door trim.

The Royale coupés were all but identical to the Opel Monzas they shared the Rüsselheim production line with. Apart from obvious badge differences, the Monza had smaller bumper overriders, and its rear numberplate was housed between the rear lights — similar to the Manta coupé, Kadett and Ascona models. The Monza, which sold for about £1000 more, had the 3-litre straight-six later offered as an option on the Royale. This Royale would have cost around £9500 in mid-1979 (it actually cost the author only £1350 in 1988!)

Above left: The Senator of the mid-1980s had an interesting history. Basically it was a revamped Royale saloon, but had been the Opel Senator since the Royale's disappearance (except for a few months' interval). A new interior, dash, and a more streamlined front end had revitalized Vauxhall's top model, which was now available with either the 2.5-litre (ex-Viceroy) or 3-litre (ex-Royale/Monza/early Senator) straight-six engines. Its beginnings dated back to the start of the V car series, the Opel Monza/Commodore/Rekord and Senator of 1978. *Above right:* With more models to choose from, the October 1982 Carlton was essentially a clever revamp of its forerunner. Look closely at those doors — the whole passenger compartment is identical in shape to the earlier series. As with the L types of the late 1940s, Vauxhall again (or in this case the styling shop in Germany) created a new car by grafting a new and this time bigger rear and front end on to an existing design. Chrome had by now all but gone, and once again Opel marketed a clone Rekord model on the Continent only. L, GL, and CD models were marketed, together with estates and diesel version complete with a necessary bonnet bulge.

The direct alternative to the Ford Capri, the Cavalier coupé (in Opel Manta guise) lasted through to 1989. One of the first few examples built here, is seen in Pastel Beige, apparently the only colour available for coupés at the start of production. The coupé (this one was photographed in Suffolk in 1988) sat a little lower than its saloon counterparts and used the more angular rear lamp clusters, similar to those found on the Triumph Stag. The Crayford Centaur — a targa-top specialist conversion — was based on the coupé body style, and was marketed in the late 1970s.

Above left: *The Belgian-built Cavalier came in four body styles two-door, four-door (shown here — minus hubcaps), two-door coupé and two-door sportshatch. No estate was offered, even by Adam Opel in West Germany. This is the 1600L, popular with fleet buyers in the mid- and late 1970s. In Britain the Cavalier easily outsold the previously available Opel Ascona by six to one, and did much to revitalize Vauxhall's ageing range when deliveries started in January 1976. Original engines were all Opel 1600s and 1900s, the latter being replaced by the Carlton 2-litre unit in the spring of 1978. A somewhat underpowered "economy" 1256 cc Chevette/Viva unit appeared in the guise of the 1300L in August 1977 — this engine was not available in Opel versions.* *Above right:* *While compiling this book, the author was lucky enough to have use of this then newly available 1987 Cavalier GLi hatchback 2-litre. This is certainly a car that begs to be driven hard, and it can certainly perform. Unfortunately it suffers from its lack of power-assisted steering which proves exceptionally heavy when parking. The car is photographed on the banks of the River Orwell, Suffolk. In the background stands the 4265 ft Orwell bridge, which was the longest pre-stressed concrete span in the United Kingdom when opened in December 1982. The carriageway is 154 ft above the highwater mark.*

"Who said tomorrow never comes?" was the sales motto for "The Car of the Future", the Cavalier 3. Heavily advertised in the press and on television, the new model Cavalier arrived boldly in 1988, and clever marketing ensured that everyone knew about it. Advertisements featured a mock 1957 dream car, with, of course, all the features of the new Cavalier. The model shown here is a new four-wheel-drive Cavalier L, pioneering the way forwards for transmission systems for family saloons. No longer was four-wheel drive for specialist and off-road vehicles.

Vauxhall's first GTE (the GTE designation originally came from the Reliant Scimitar of the 1960s) appeared in the form of the Mark 1 Astra, a medium-to small-sized "hot hatch" as they became known in the 1980s, in strong competition with Ford's Escort XR3. Its 1796 cc 115 bhp engine could push the Astra to an impressive 116 mph when launched, in the spring of 1983. As with the XR3 and Golf GTi — probably its strongest opposition — the Astra was available in three-door hatch form only. Note the modest transfer badge on the front wing, and the black window surround treatment, à la Ford XR3 of 1981.

The Mark 2 Astra GTE started life as a 1.8-litre in 1984, and even this 115 bhp version could reach 125 mph, a credit to its ultra-smooth flowing lines that owed so much to its wind tunnel testing. Aerodynamically, the GTE was the most efficient of the new Astras, aided by its deep front and rear spoilers; a Cd figure of just 0.32 was achieved. Unusually, Vauxhall produced some four-door models of the 1.8 GTE, but not of the following 2-litre version, which was later given the option of 16 valves during 1988. The rather glossy brochure of 1988 enthusiastically stated that, "in neutral conditions — no wind, no gradient — its maximum speed is 137 mph". The car pictured is a 2-litre.

The Rüsselsheim-built Senator 2 of 1987 in 2490 or 2969 cc injection form, Vauxhall's most luxurious model to date. Based on the new Carlton/Opel Omega from the previous year, the super-slick Senator was a welcome improvement on its ageing forerunner. Standard equipment includes ABS, fully independent suspension, automatic transmission, computerized dashboard, metallic paint, six in-car entertainment speakers, heated and height-adjustable seats, and a whole host of electronic gadgetry. Naturally, the new Senator sits nicely in the BMW/Mercedes/Jaguar/Rover market and is popular with managing directors.

This is the one-off 2300 Sportshatch Firenza "Silver Bullet", produced by Wayne Cherry as a styling exercise, photographed 1988. Note the unusual six headlamp treatment in the "droop snoot" front end. The car has been lovingly restored by Vauxhall enthusiasts Mario and Edmund Lindsay, who have vowed never to sell this masterpiece. They also own the Cavalier 1 Sportshatch "Silver Aero", featured elsewhere. It can be confirmed that both of these cars are in superb running order, and thankfully look set to remain in good hands for many years to come.

112

Below: A practical conversion of the little HA van of 1967 was the Roma, by Dormobile, first shown at the 1967 London Motor Show. It came soon after Martin Walter's Beagle estate car conversion based on the same vehicle. Visible here is the elevating fibreglass roof section. The two-sleeper interior featured a hanging cupboard and gas cooker (the author wonders where it all fitted, with the Bedford's length of 12 ft 11 in). A more sensible family solution, perhaps, was the Romany, based on the Bedford CA van, two of which are visible here. The history of motor caravans does not go back as far as one might think. Research indicates that Martin Walter of Folkestone, Kent was probably the first, with their £785 Dormobile conversion on the Bedford CA 15 cwt (with sliding doors) in 1958. The converted CA van was a four-berth affair with elevating roof and was powered by the contemporary Victor 1½ litre engine, albeit in low compression form. Performance was a reasonable 70 mph, 0–50 mph in 25 sec, and an overall fuel consumption of 26 mpg.

Above: Between the Firenza/Magnum HC models of the early 1970s and the Manta/Cavalier coupé of the early and mid-1980s, the Chevette was a common sight in many rallies. The "homologation special" was the 2300S. This featured a 16-valve cylinder head in a bodyshell little altered from standard, except for deep spoilers and massively extended wheel arches. The transmission included a heavy duty back axle, and a much-needed German five-speed Getrag gearbox. The motoring press highlighted the confusion about whether or not the 400 models had been manufactured — essential for entry into RAC rallies. In the end 400 were made, all in silver, of which about 50 were converted in to the even faster HSR, as photographed here at Snetterton in early 1988. This very lively Chevette belongs to Terry Cobbold of the Droop Snoot Group.

mornings). A number of limited editions were made available in the early 1980s, no doubt a reminder that the Chevette was still very much around, even though it may have been overshadowed by the Astra I, with which it shared the production line from late 1981. Gradually the model range was decreased to a mere trickle until 12 March 1985 when production number 415,630 rolled off the Ellesmere Port line as the last Chevette — a four-door saloon — nine years after the introduction of the series.

NOVA

Punchy, zippy, fun and economical were some of the adjectives applied to the little front-wheel-drive Nova launched in the spring of 1983, described by the firm itself as "engineered for rugged dependability".

The Nova was part of General Motors' S car concept, first rumoured in the late 1970s. Unlike the first Cavalier, the Carlton and the 1975 Chevette, it joined the modern trend in receiving very little in the way of design changes to earn itself its individual Vauxhall badge. Three small cars were now marketed by the company: at Ellesmere Port there were the Astra and Chevette models, the latter (the company's only all-British product) was really in its run-down period by now; and there was the Spanish-built Nova. The Nova had been on sale in France and Spain since October 1982 as the Opel Corsa, and when launched in Britain was marketed heavily to compete with home-produced Fiestas and Metros. Thanks to its British family name, and despite being assembled abroad, the Nova sold well, initially in three-door hatch, and two-door saloon styles. Interestingly, the two-door saloon was actually cheaper than the hatch model. This proved popular with both small dog owners (who did not relish the idea of their pets jumping out of an open tailgate at the first opportunity), and die-hards who wanted a cheap conventional vehicle: the Nova was the cheapest such car around, except for a handful of old-fashioned East European models. At first glance it was not easy to see the family resemblance between saloon and hatch: the models not only had different grilles, but different front and rear wing mouldings too. The model line-up included base models, the Ls, and the sporty model of the range was the five-speed SR, with a 100 mph+ performance from its 1.3-litre engine. The limited edition Nova Sport was a homologation special, and was not built in any significant numbers. The base-with-a-difference Merit and GL models also joined the fleet later on.

The rather chunky Nova hatch, this one in five-door 1.3GL form, dating to 1986. Note the more conventional wheel arches — compare this photo to the two-door hatch in the colour picture, page 107. It would not have been aesthetically pleasing for the styling shop to have incorporated the boxed arches of the three-door hatch into the five-door derivative, nor to have mixed the two types together. The Nova came in 1-, 1.2-, 1.3-, and special 1.6-litre fuel-injected GTE forms, all with very precise handling and impressive mpg figures. The name was far from new it dates back to the early 1970s when Chevrolet had marketed its Nova, which unfortunately suffered a bad reliability reputation in the States.

Soon, a remarkable five-door hatch arrived, as well as a five-door saloon, which looked for all the world like a scaled-down Senator. At the time of writing the Nova has enjoyed a seven-year production run, and still takes a respectable slice of the home market.

Regional marketing was applied in late 1988: the special editions listed in the table were only available in certain areas of the country — the Swing in the south of England for example.

In 1988, the Nova GTE arrived, a fully colour-co-ordinated new sports model to compete with the ageing Mark 1 XR2 Fiesta and MG Metro Turbo models. The writer is yet to secure a drive in one of these beasts — but is assured that this "pocket rocket" is very quick and can leave most other traffic standing! In an attempt to rival the new Ford Fiesta XR2, Vauxhall, in 1990, standardized certain options previously available, such as power-operated windows.

London's Motor Fair 1989 was the platform used to first display the Nova 1.5TD (Turbo Diesel), a modest Merit hatchback model that could achieve a commendable 70.6 mpg at a constant 56 mph. "Every Nova 1.5TD comes with a rev counter as standard, incidentally, so you can keep an eye on exactly what your engine's up to", said the sales blurb.

The tail end of 1990 saw a major facelift to the Nova — the "Euro-car" rounded look now fully in evidence. The GTE was renamed the GSi and two-door saloons were deleted from the price lists. A brand new Nova? — not until 1993.

Launched in 1983 and built in Spain, the Nova was still a strong contender in the British market as this book closed for press. Here is the Nova four-door saloon, its unrivalled-at-the-price three-box design popular with customers on a budget needing a conventional saloon body, but not wanting to buy a foreign car (although that is what it is!). If you squint long enough, particularly at a two-door version, its three-box proportions are very similar to those of the Viva HA of 1963.

Model	Nova
Dates of Production	April 1983 to current
Body Types	2-door saloon; 3-door hatchback;
	5-door hatchback; 4-door saloon
Engines Offered	993 cc, 1196 cc, 1297 cc (70 bhp)
	1389 cc, 1488 cc (diesel) 1598 cc
Transmission	Manual 4- and 5-speed automatic
Average Fuel Consumption	35-45 mpg
Mpg at 56 mph	From 51 mpg (GTE) to 70-76 mpg
	(1.5 TD)
Top Speed	89 mph (1.0 litre) to 117 mph (GTE)
Braking System	Dual circuit, servo-assisted, disc front,
	drums rear
Wheels and Tyres	Wheels: $4\frac{1}{2}$J x 13; (GTE has 5J x 14);
	tyres: 14SSR13 165/70 TR
	(GTE: 175/65 HR14)
Dimensions	Length: 12 ft $11\frac{7}{10}$ in (saloon);
	11 ft 10 in (hatch); width: 5 ft $0\frac{6}{10}$ in
	(saloon), 5 ft 0 in (hatch);
	height: 4 ft $5\frac{1}{2}$ in (saloon),
	4ft $5\frac{7}{10}$ in (hatch)
Weight	1631-1839 lb
Price at Launch	£3496
Drag Co-efficient	Cd 0.37 (GTE); Cd 0.36 (SR);
	Cd 0.38 (saloon); Cd 0.37 (hatch)
Made in	Spain
Number Produced	N/A
Also available as	Opel Corsa

116

The 1.6 Nova GTE has all the cheek of the Mini Cooper S of two and a half decades ago. It is small, fast, and downright fun to drive! Unlike the Mini, it will take four in reasonable peace and comfort, and was capable of returning over 50 mpg on unleaded fuel. For the 1991 model year, the GTE was replaced by the GSi. Photograph Linden Lait.

Model	Engine	From	To
CHEVETTE			
Chevette hatch	1256	3/75	4/76
Chevette L hatch	1256	3/75	1984
Chevette GL hatch	1256	10/75	1983
Chevette E saloon 2-door	1256	1/76	9/82
Chevette E saloon 4-door	1256	1/76	9/82
Chevette GLS hatch	1256	4/76	1978
Chevette E hatch	1256	6/76	9/82
Chevette L saloon 2-door	1256	6/76	8/83
Chevette L saloon 4-door	1256	6/76	1984
Chevette GLS saloon 4-door	1256	6/76	3/78
Chevette L estate 3-door	1256	9/76	1984
Chevette 2300HS hatch	2279	1/78	1979
Chevette GL saloon 4-door	1256	10/78	8/83
Chevette Starlight Limited Edition	1256	11/78	–
Chevette Midnight Limited Edition	1256	11/78	–
Chevette 2300HSR	2279	1979	1981
Chevette Regatta hatch Limited Edition	1256	1979	–
Chevette Black Magic (one-off)	2279	9/79	–
Chevette Special (1) 2-door Limited Edition	1256	3/80	–
Chevette Special (1) 4-door Limited Edition	1256	3/80	–
Chevette E estate	1256	4/80	9/82
Chevette Sunhatch Limited Edition	1256	6/80	–
Chevette ES hatch	1256	10/80	9/82
Chevette ES saloon 2-door	1256	10/80	9/82
Chevette Command Performance hatch Limited Edition	1256	11/80	–

Chevette Black Pearl Limited Edition	1256	4/81	–
Chevette Special (2) saloon 2-door	1256	11/81	–
Chevette Special (2) saloon 4-door	1256	11/81	–
Chevette Special (2) saloon hatch	1256	11/81	–
Chevette Silhouette hatch Limited Edition	1256	4/82	–

NOVA

Nova 1.0 saloon 2-door	993	4/83	10/90
Nova 1.0 hatch 3-door	993	4/83	10/90
Nova 1.2 L saloon 2-door	1196	4/83	1987
Nova 1.2 L hatch 3-door	1196	4/83	current
Nova SR hatch 3-door	1297	4/83	10/89
Nova 1.0 L saloon 2-door	993	10/83	1986
Nova 1.0 L hatch 3-door	993	10/83	1986
Nova 1.2 saloon 2-door	1196	10/83	1986
Nova 1.2 hatch 3-door	1196	10/83	1986
Nova 1.2 GL saloon 2-door	1196	1/84	1986
Nova 1.2 GL hatch 3-door	993	1/84	1986
Nova Swing hatch 3-door Limited Edition	993	5/84	–
Nova Swing hatch 3-door Limited Edition	1196	5/84	–
Nova Sport hatch 3-door Limited Edition	1297	1/85	–
Nova Merit hatch 3-door	993	5/85	1988
Nova Merit 1.2 saloon 2-door	1196	5/85	10/90
Nova Merit 1.2 saloon 4-door	1196	5/85	current
Nova Merit 1.2 hatch 3-door	1196	5/85	current
Nova Merit 1.2 hatch 5-door	1196	5/85	current
Nova 1.2 L saloon 4-door	1196	5/85	current
Nova 1.2 L hatch 5-door	1196	5/85	current
Nova 1.3 L saloon 4-door	1297	5/85	10/89
Nova 1.3 GL saloon 4-door	1297	5/85	1987
Nova 1.3 GL hatch 5-door	1297	5/85	1987
Nova Antibes hatch 3-door Limited Edition	1196	5/86	–
Nova 1.0 hatch 5-door	993	8/86	1988
Casa Nova hatch 3-door Limited Edition	1196	1987	–
Nova Club hatch 3-door	1196	4/87	–
Nova Antibes (relaunch) hatch 3-door	1196	7/87	–
Nova 1.3 L hatch 5-door	1297	8/87	10/89
Nova GTE	1598	6/88	10/90
Nova Gem hatch 3-door Limited Edition	993	6/88	–
Nova Diamond hatch 3-door Limited Edition	1196	6/88	–
Nova Swing 3-door Limited Edition	993	10/88	–
Nova 1.3 L saloon 3-door	1297	1988	10/89
Nova Flair 3-door Limited Edition	1196	1/89	–

Nova Pearl 3-door Limited Edition	1297	6/89	–
Nova Star hatch 3-door Limited Edition	1196	6/89	–
Nova Sting 3-door Limited Edition	1196	9/89	–
Nova SR hatch 3-door	1389	10/89	current
Nova 1.4 Merit hatch 3-door	1389	10/89	current
Nova 1.4 Merit saloon 4-door	1389	10/89	current
Nova 1.4 Merit hatch 5-door	1389	10/89	current
Nova 1.4 L hatch 3-door	1389	10/89	current
Nova 1.4 L saloon 4-door	1389	10/89	current
Nova 1.4 L hatch 5-door	1389	10/89	current
Nova 1.5 Turbo Diesel	1488	11/89	current
Nova Fling hatch 3-door Limited Edition	993	6/90	–
Nova Diamond hatch 3-door Limited Edition	993	6/90	–
Nova GSI	1598	10/90	current
Nova Trip hatch 3-door	993	10/90	current
Nova Trip saloon 4-door	993	10/90	current
Nova Flair hatch 3-door	1196	10/90	current
Nova Flair hatch 3-door	1389	10/90	current

8

The V cars

Mass "Opelization" brought the V cars to Vauxhall in late 1978. British eyes had been used to the then new, large and attractive four-cylinder Opel Rekord models for over a year, in both their two-door (never to be seen on the Luton-built Carlton) and four-door form. The Vauxhall versions retained the now familiar sloping "droop snoot" nose treatment, this time a little more angular, and those bonnet flutes were continued from the now defunct FE series. Power came at 2 litres only — the same Opel engine/gearbox that was used in the top Cavalier models some months earlier. To simplify production there were just two models to choose from: a saloon and an estate. Apart from minor trim modifications, the Mark 1 Carltons continued largely unchanged until October 1982, when the Mark 2 was introduced at the Motor Show. One cannot help wondering if the Carlton was never the success it was meant to be: in the first five years just over 27,000 were manufactured.

Designed on the same floorpan, and sharing many components, were the luxuriously appointed Royale saloon and coupé models. It was no secret that these were clones of the Opel Senator and Monza models respectively, except for the smaller engine (at least initially). The Vauxhalls were built at Rüsselsheim, West Germany, alongside their German kin: the small differences are given elsewhere.

The first 70 Monzas and Senators were completed and running in prototype form in September 1977 (indeed when the smaller four-cylinder Opel-badged versions had originally been announced) and were exhibited publicly for the first time at the Frankfurt Motor Show, to test public reaction. Reaction was better than expected: the silver saloon and coupé models attracted more attention than the seemingly outdated and dumpy BMW 7 series displayed opposite. Although Ford would never dream of such unusual marketing moves, Vauxhall and Opel Royale and Senator/Monza models were sold in tandem in Britain until late 1982, when all six-cylinder Vauxhall models were discontinued in favour of the Opels. In 1980 the optional 3-litre engine became available in the Vauxhall Royale and the Opels took on board the less powerful 2.8, although German specification cars had had a 2.8 version from the start. Both units were of Opel origin, dating back to the late 1960s. The no extra cost optional four-speed manual gearbox became a five-speeder, shortly before the rebadging took place, and the better Opel-style dash moulding was adopted for the Royale. Apart from the no-cost choice of manual transmission, virtually the only option available to Royale customers was air conditioning — everything else was standard. The Royale coupé, with its production run of a mere 3500 or so, is a rare sight on Britain's roads today. Two owners clubs were established in 1990 for this exclusive vehicle.

The 1980 Motor Show saw an unusual car exhibited by Vauxhall for the first time. This was the Viceroy, a strange combination of Royale front end, complete with six-cylinder engine (this time the 2490 cc straight six, originally employed in the 1967 Commodore), and Carlton rear, with the Carlton's live rear axle, but the Royale's five-stud hubs! Adding to the interest of this very low-volume car (just over 2000 were produced) was the white cross motif on the front, very similar to that on earlier VX 4/90 models and the "strobe-decal-striping" above the body side moulding. Again, the interior was a combination of Carlton trim and basically the Royale dash, although it lacked the adjustable steering column and some electrical features of the latter car. Despite the

Destined to replace the rapidly ageing FE Transcontinental range, the British-built Carlton of October 1978 was largely similar to its German cousins the Opel Rekords and Commodores except for detail badging, dash changes, chunkier bumpers and, of course, the by now customary "droop snoot" trade mark previously used on the HP Firenza and subsequently on Chevettes and Cavaliers. The "droop snoot" helped the drag factor. Much design work undertaken at Stuttgart University had been concentrated on keeping this to a minimum. Power came from the Opel 1979 cc four-cylinder unit, already in use for some seven months in the Cavalier. A high specification was offered with the Carlton, but despite this it was not a good seller and only 27,488 were produced in four years less than a fifth of the total FE production.

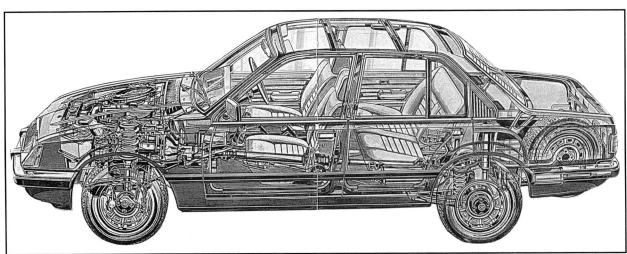

Model	Carlton 1 & 2
Dates of Production	October 1978 to October 1986
Body Types	4 door-saloon; 5-door estate
Engines Offered	1979 cc; 1796 cc; 2197 cc; 2260 cc diesel
Transmission	Manual 4-speed (5 with facelift); optional 3-speed automatic
Average Fuel Consumption Mpg at 56 mph	24 mpg (2-litre); 28 mpg (1.8-litre) 38.7 mpg (saloon, manual); 36.7 mpg (estate, manual); 32.8 mpg (saloon, auto); 33.6 mpg (estate, auto)
Top Speed	107 mph (manual 2000 cc saloon)
0-60 Mph	11.4 sec (2000 cc)
Braking System	Dual-circuit, servo-assisted, front disc, rear drums
Wheels and Tyres	Wheels: $5\frac{1}{2}$J x 14 ventilated steel; tyres: 175SR x 14 radial
Dimensions	Length: 15 ft $6\frac{7}{10}$ in (saloon); 15 ft $6\frac{3}{10}$ in (estate); width: 5 ft 8 in; height: 4 ft $5\frac{1}{2}$ in (saloon); 4 ft $8\frac{1}{3}$ in estate
Weight	2486 lb (2-litre saloon); 2596 lb (estate)
Production Changes	October 1982: extensive facelift, new front & rear ends, plastic bumpers, Opel dashboard layout, new seats, 5-speed manual gearbox; additional range of engines available
Price at Launch	£4600 (saloon); £5068 (estate)
Made at	Luton
Number Produced	27,000 earlier models (1978-82) 53,000 later models (1982-6)
Also available as	Opel Rekord

smaller engine, acceleration was well ahead of its lumbering big brother Royale models — even the sporty coupé. It was helped, no doubt, by its 15 per cent lighter body; although the top speed of the larger-engined Royales was better. However, only a saloon was produced (although there is evidence of plans of what would have been a nice rival to the Volvo 265 estate) and it was included in the price lists for precisely two years. For when Opel cars joined forces with the Vauxhalls in the same sales catalogues, the West German-built Viceroy was dropped almost immediately in favour of the nearly identical Opel Commodore Berlina, and the more luxurious Commodore Berlina CD, which had been available in Germany since autumn 1978. Because of its low volume of production the Viceroy could become a modern-day collector's car.

When the modernized "plastic ended" Mark 2 Carltons were announced at the 1982 Motor Show, there was to be no six-cylinder model, at least for a while. However, the restyled Senator soon returned, still in Opel guise, this time without the bonnet flutes that it and the Royale had shared. Noticeable was the more aerodynamic front and rear ends and the now dated chrome bumpers had gone. There was now the choice of either the 127 mph, 3- or the 2.5-litre six. In September 1984 its name was changed from Opel to Vauxhall, and the model continued virtually unaltered until its demise three years later.

The Mark 2 Carltons were basically the earlier Carltons with an extensive facelift. They owed their more aerodynamic shape to the experimental Opel Tech 1. The Cd figure achieved was a respectable 0.36. The most striking change was to the front, which adopted the now familiar "egg crate" grille, bigger, more angular headlamps, and a deep spoiler. However, the saloon's rear had larger, fatter lamp clusters with the numberplate mounted between them (it had been fitted in a specific slot on the bumper previously). The estate version remained remarkably similar in shape, but with clever additional chromework looked more up-market. There were no fewer than ten models in the original range, and more engines to choose from, including a 2.3-litre diesel (complete with the necessary bonnet bulge) and the CD badge was fitted to top line saloons. Although mechanically similar in other areas — Mark 2s were given a five-speed gearbox — and even the optional automatic had a "lock-up" in top gear. The Mark 2 Carlton proved more successful than its predecessors. On the Continent, a virtually identical Opel Rekord was sold.

It is certainly worthy of mention here that these V cars are still extremely popular with enthusiasts in Australia. The Holden Commodore (VB), launched in late 1978, was basically an Australian Viceroy/Commodore, available with a variety of engines, from a 3.3-litre six to two V8s (4200 cc and 5000 cc). In fact, this model won Australia's *Wheels* magazine "Car of the Year" award. A while later the Senator/Royale-like Holden (the VK called the Calais or Executive) arrived on the scene with similar awesome power. An active club for would-be "street-racers" exists in Australia; and the writer's contact there insists that you are not highly "street-credible" if you do not drive a Holden V8!

A group of the new V cars were taken to London for photographic purposes early in October 1978. Here a Carlton estate is seen crossing Westminster Bridge, with Big Ben and the Houses of Parliament in the background. It would have been a strange sight for any car enthusiast, for it would appear, at a distance to have been an Opel Rekord with sloping nose cone; the Rekord had already made its début in Britain nine months earlier.

Quite clear here are the traditional Vauxhall bonnet flutes, a nice touch carried on after the discontinuation of the FE range. Note the headrests, now even available in this mid-range family car.

There are rumours that the original prototype Holden V8 Commodore — a German model — actually snapped in two during rigorous testing (ahead of the bulkhead). The V8's delivery of power proved too much for the West German-designed body.

A rather limited edition Holden Calais (which sold at up to about $45,000 with all options) was called the Calais Director, and makes a Vauxhall Senator seem dull in comparison. Australia's *Modern Motor* road-tested a Calais Director in May 1986 and achieved the following results: 0–100 km/h (62 mph) in 6.91 seconds, standard quarter = 14.78 seconds, and a top speed of 242 km/h (150 mph). Unlike the VBs, which were also built as estates, these VK series of cars were available in four-door saloon type only.

Somewhat exaggerated by the camera's wide-angle lens, we see the interior of the Carlton Mark 1 estate, with rear seats in upright position. The offside wheel arch is elongated in order to house the petrol filler tube. Although a Viceroy estate was never produced, this would probably have been the view from the rear if it had. Indeed, owners of early Viceroys noted that the Owner's Manual made mention of a non-existent estate version all the way through! The ventilation slots in the rear actually house the standard-equipment radio speakers; a third speaker was located under the centre of the facia. The Carlton estate had a load capacity of some 1300 lb; the cargo space with the rear seat up was 3 ft 9 in long, extending to 6 ft 5 in with it down. A van version of the Carlton was never produced, although Opel sold its Rekord van in Britain during the late 1970s. The Chevette and HA were the only car-derived vans in the Bedford line-up until 1981. The little HA vehicle was then replaced by the more modern front-wheel-drive Astra van.

The 1979 cc so called cam-in-head Mark 1 Carlton engine, as quickly adopted for the Mark 1 Cavaliers and already in use by Opel's Rekord. No diesel Carlton Mark 1 was ever produced, but Opel offered a 2068 cc diesel Rekord (a noisy engine and huge bonnet bulge identify it), soon to be increased to 2.3-litres.

Top left: *The interior of the earliest Carltons, this one in four-speed manual format. Basically, the same dash moulding was used as on the Royale and later Viceroy, until a last-minute change into line with Opel Commodore, Senator, Monza and Rekord models shortly before production ceased. However, instead of the four small supplementary gauges found on the six-cylinder vehicles, the Carlton had just two, and a large clock took the place of the rev counter found on its six-cylinder sisters. Interestingly, a full Royale dash could have been ordered as an official option, so that the clock moved to the large, and now ugly, blanking panel over towards the left. A radio (just visible) was standard equipment, one speaker located under the centre of the dash, and one under each corner of the parcel shelf. The hazard warning button is visible on the top of the steering column.*
Above right: *The disappearance of the top-of-the-range VX 2300GLS in summer 1978 meant there was no top luxury model, at least for a while. The gap was filled at the October 1978 London Motor Show with the introduction of the Opel Monza/-Senator look-alikes the Rüsselsheim-built Royale coupé and saloons respectively, being the most luxuriously equipped Vauxhalls ever. Here is the lavish interior of a Royale saloon (this is not a well-educated guess there are* four *electric window switches visible on the centre console of this picture). Seen behind the right-hand gap in the steering wheel is the control lever for the rather clever height-adjustable steering column. Compare this picture with the cheaper Carlton Mark 1 dash. Extensive "Opelization" meant that later Viceroys, Royales and Carltons (from September 1981) had the Rekord/Commodore dash moulding for a short while. Note no fewer than three horn controls on the steering wheel.*

Model	Royale
Dates of Production	October 1978 to February 1982
Body Types	4-door saloon; 2-door coupé
Engines Offered	2784 cc (138 bhp) 6-cylinder: optional
	2968 cc (177 bhp) 6-cylinder
Transmission	3-speed auto; manual 4- or 5-speed (no-cost option)
Average Fuel Consumption	17-25 mpg
Mpg at 56 mph	33mpg (2.8 manual 5-speed); 35 mpg (30 manual 5-speed); 29 mpg (2.8 auto); 28 mpg (3.0 auto)
Top Speed	113 mph (saloon); 117 mph (coupé)
	125 mph (3.0 coupé) (All figures for auto transmission)
0-60 Mph	11.4 sec (2.8-litre automatic)
Braking System	Dual circuit, servo-assisted, discs all round
Wheels and Tyres	Wheels: 6J x 14; tyres: 195/70 HR
Dimensions	Length: 16 ft (saloon), 15 ft 7$\frac{3}{10}$ in (coupé); width: 5 ft 8 in, height: 4 ft 5$\frac{4}{5}$ in (saloon), 4 ft 4$\frac{1}{2}$ in (coupé)
Weight	3164 lb, saloon; 3175 lb coupé
Production Changes	April 1980: 5-speed manual optional; October 1980: 3-litre injection optional; basically unchanged until October 1981, when Opel Monza dashboard layout adopted, rear wash wipe added, on-board computer and front spoiler bib added
Price at Launch	£7956 (saloon); £8248 (coupé)
Made at	Rüsselsheim, West Germany
Number Produced	7525 only
Also available as	Opel Monza (coupé); Opel Senator Mk 1 (saloon); Holden Commodore VK (saloon)

The long and sleek look of the Royale coupé proved very attractive to British eyes, so much so that the author believes this vehicle to be a Vauxhall classic of the future. Astro silver metallic AVS 62T, Vauxhall's early press car, is suitably located outside Buckingham Palace, early in October 1978. The Royale was then the only Vauxhall fully assembled abroad, at the Adam Opel factory in Rüsselsheim, even down to detail badging. The full complement of equipment was so comprehensive that just two options were listed in the sales brochures no cost manual transmission and air conditioning. The Royales brought the delights of six-cylinder motoring back to Vauxhall, after almost three years since the passing of the Ventora. The best performance equation was the later 3.0 injection manual version; 0-60 mph in 8.5 sec.

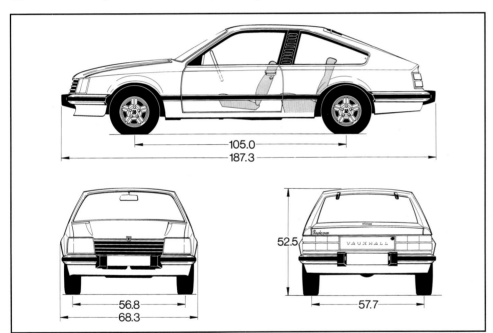

The Royale coupé models were nearly 5 in shorter and fractionally lower and wider (although the author is baffled by the latter) than sister saloon models. Notice how the line drawing of the front of the vehicle looks so very much like the earlier BL Princess!

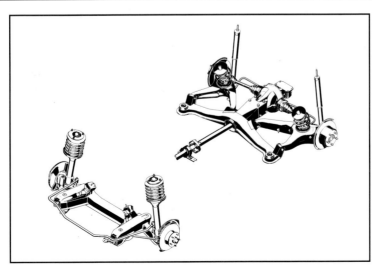

Now of course very dated, the fully independent suspension system of the Royale saloon and coupé models was somewhat revolutionary in the late 1970s — it was Vauxhall's first dabble with IRS systems. Note the McPherson struts at the front.

While the Viceroy was shortlived; the "Phase 2" version passed by almost unnoticed. Announced at the 1980 London Motor Show, and manufactured between early 1981 and February 1982, most of the Viceroys on the road (just over 2000 were produced) appear to be in the earlier guise. Phase 2 revisions coincided with those of the other V cars and included black side window surrounds; more stream-lined door mirrors; central locking; Opel dash (now, shamefully, with no more wood veneer included); striped seats and door trims; and a rubber strip mounted at the base of the spoiler — à la XR3. Note the VX 4/90-style white cross — a trademark unique to Vauxhall that made the car instantly recognizable from any distance. The body style remained the same basically a Carlton from the A posts back (albeit with extra chrome), and Royale from the A posts forward. The 15-year-old 2490 cc straight-six Opel power unit continued. Note that a Buick Viceroy had existed many years earlier — that com-pany's most spartan model of the time!

Model	Viceroy
Dates of Production	October 1980 to February 1982
Body Types	4-door saloon only
Engines Offered	2490 cc (114 bhp)
Transmission	4-speed manual (optional, then stan-dard overdrive); or optional 3-speed automatic
Average Fuel Consumption	18-24 mpg
Mpg at 56 mph	33.2 mpg (manual); 34.4 mpg (over-drive); 29.7 mpg (automatic)
Top Speed	110 mph (manual); 107 mph (auto)
0-60 Mph	10.7 sec (automatic)
Braking System	Dual circuit, servo-assisted
Wheels and Tyres	Wheels: 6J x 14; tyres: 175 HR x 14 radial
Dimensions	Length: 15 ft $7\frac{1}{2}$ in; width: 5 ft $7\frac{7}{10}$ in; height: 4 ft $5\frac{1}{2}$ in
Weight	2712 lb
Production Changes	Phase 2 Viceroy from October 1981: black window surrounds, better interior trim, "wooden" dash disappears, streamlined mirrors, front spoiler bib, electronic ignition
Price at Launch	£7864
Made at	Rüsselsheim, West Germany
Number Produced	2295 only
Also available as	Opel Commodore and similar Holden Commodore VB

A maximum 120 mph, clean straight lines and a full luxury specification brought the late 1978 Royale models into the 1980s. For the first time on a Vauxhall-badged car (although, of course, far from new in concept) there was independent rear suspension. Initially available with a 2.8-litre (ex-Opel) straight-six engine and then the larger optional 3-litre six, the Royale boasted three-speed automatic transmission as standard equipment (although manual could be ordered as a special no extra cost option). The top-tinted windscreen and headlamp washers (activated in tandem with the windscreen washers) were also standard fitting. No Royale estate — or Opel equivalent — was ever built perhaps owners of Granada estates, Volvo estates or even Range Rovers could have been lured away . . . This Rüsselsheim-built car, albeit with detail changes, continued for several years after rationalization in February 1982 meant that six-cylinder Vauxhalls were replaced by Opels, in this particular case the Senator. (Opel had been marketing its version as the Senator since early 1978.)

Below left and right: Carlton Mark 2s were simply rebadged Opel Rekords. The new shape Carlton boasted a more windcheating shape than its predecessor, and the chrome bumpers had disappeared. This is the GL saloon, with dealer-fitted mudflaps.

Left: The Carlton Mark 2 estate was a direct competitor to the popular Volvo estates. It came in a choice of five engines, including this, the 2.3-litre diesel. The model was distinguished easily by the bonnet bulge, shown quite clearly in this photo.

Quite simply, the Senator of 1985 looked like a Royale of previous years, except that this model had a new front and rear grafted on, and power came in at 2.5- or 3-litres. Originally, the Senator belonged to the Opel stable, but the marketing department strangely changed it to the Vauxhall badge in the mid-1980s.

Model	Senator 1
Dates of Production	October 1984 (from 2/83 as Opel) to October 1987
Body Types	4-door saloon
Engines Offered	2490 cc, 2968 cc, both 6-cylinder
Transmission	5-speed manual; 3- then 4-speed automatic
Average Fuel Consumption	19 mpg
Mpg at 56 mph	38.2 mpg (2490 cc manual); 37.1 mpg (automatic); 37.1 mpg (2968 cc manual); 37.7 mpg (automatic)
Top Speed	118 mph (2.5 auto); 130 mph (3.0 manual)
0-60 Mph	9.7 sec (3.0 manual)
Braking System	Dual circuit, servo-assisted, front disc, rear disc
Wheels and Tyres	Wheels: 6J x 14; tyres 195/70 VR or HR low profile
Dimensions	Length: 15 ft 10½ in; width: 5 ft 7⅘ in; height: 4 ft 7$\frac{7}{10}$ in
Weight	3045 lb
Production Changes	Rebadged from Opel Senator
Price at Launch	£13,994
Made at	Rüsselsheim, West Germany
Number Produced	N/A

One Viceroy on the roads these days is a rarity (and the author notes that they never seem to be present at any owners' meetings), but two is a real novelty. Pictured here in Sussex are two 1981 examples (the author's vehicle is at the front) with their contemporary rival, the Rover SD1.

Vauxhall's version of the Opel Commodore, the Viceroy. Because of their scarcity and unnecessary thirst, the Viceroy seems now to have all but disappeared from British roads. Many were automatic, complementing the six-cylinder 2490 cc engine, which is basically still offered in the Senator today. This charming setting is Bodiam Castle in Sussex.

Model	Engine	From	To
V CARS			
Carlton saloon	1979	10/78	10/82
Carlton estate	1979	10/78	10/82
Royale saloon	2784	10/78	2/82
Royale coupé	2784	10/78	2/82
Royale saloon (optional 3.0)	2968	10/80	2/82
Royale coupé (optional 3.0)	2968	10/80	2/82
Viceroy (saloon only)	2490	10/80	2/82
Carlton Command Performance saloon	1979	11/80	–
Carlton saloon	1796	10/82	6/83
Carlton estate	1796	10/82	6/83
Carlton GL	1796	10/82	10/86
Carlton GL estate	1796	10/82	10/86
Carlton saloon	1979	10/82	6/83
Carlton estate	1979	10/82	6/83
Carlton GL	1979	10/82	10/86
Carlton GL estate	1979	10/82	early 86
Carlton D	2260	10/82	6/83
Carlton L	1796	6/83	10/86
Carlton L estate	1796	6/83	10/86
Carlton L	1979	6/83	10/86
Carlton L estate	1979	6/83	10/86
Carlton L D	2260	6/83	10/86
Carlton L D estate	2260	6/83	10/86
Carlton D Estate	2260	10/82	6/83
Carlton CD saloon	1979	7/83	8/85
Carlton GL saloon	2197	8/85	10/86
Carlton GL estate	2197	8/85	10/86
Carlton CD saloon	2197	8/85	10/86
Carlton CD estate	2197	8/85	10/86
Senator *	2490	10/84	10/87
Senator *	2968	10/84	10/87
Senator CD *	2968	10/84	10/87

* previously marketed as an Opel Senator from 2/83

The Cavaliers — Popular Family Cars with Appeal

Whereas the Viva/Magnum models were too small, and the rapidly ageing FEs too big and cumbersome, the new Cavalier of November 1975 proved itself a popular car and many were sold or leased to companies for sales representatives. The Cavalier once again was based on Opel mechanical components, this time the Ascona, and was offered in either two- or four-door saloon, or two-door coupé form, this last version resembling the then new Opel Manta. The front inherited the Manta's unusual sloping nose cone, minus slats: not perhaps odd for today's eyes, of course, but quite rare for the 1970s, except for the Chevette, the Renault 5, new Rover SD1 series, and a handful of exotic sports cars.

Vauxhall soon saw a gap for an economy model and launched the Cavalier 1300, basically powered by the 1256 cc engine used in the Chevette and Viva models of the day. The sportshatch version was launched the same day as the equivalent Opel Manta, and this completed the range. Some Cavaliers made it on to the Continent; the unusually named L2 for the Belgian market, for example (where the Cavalier was built originally). Most, however, were sold in right hand drive form in Britain, with the Opels taking preference on the Continent. Nearly a quarter of a million Mark 1 Cavaliers were manufactured during the car's five-year run.

The Cavalier 2 turned into perhaps the most successful Vauxhall ever. Hence by 1982 the number of vehicles produced in a single year had risen from 117,266 (previous year) to 187,078, thanks to this car. Again, mechanical components were from the near-clone Ascona (both vehicles being part of the General Motors J car concept) and it sold worldwide under the names of Opel Ascona (West Germany), Holden Camira (Australia), Chevrolet and Buick Cavalier (USA). In Britain there was a choice of three body styles initially, but this was soon whittled down to two. The basic two-door model, aimed primarily at fleet buyers and not prominently featured in advertisements and brochures, was carried forward for one year before discontinuation. This left the five-door hatch and four-door saloon, which were soon to be accompanied by a boxy yet attractive five-door estate car, available in 1600 cc form only. The later 1800 injection cabriolet — this time designed and marketed by Vauxhall itself — was based on the original two-door car, but never sold in particularly high numbers. An owners club has recently been established dealing exclusively with these open Cavaliers.

Aesthetically the Cavalier 2 never really started to age and still looks modern today, a credit to the original design, as well as to the trim and paint schemes available on later registered examples. This is highlighted by the fact that it won the AFCO "Fleet Car of the Year" award in both 1985 and 1986, as well as the "Holiday Car of the Year", sponsored by *Motor* and *Pleasurewood Holidays*. Later models had the (originally) SRi reflective strip encompassing the number-plate on the rear, even down to the basic models. Then a new line of LX and LXi models appeared shortly before the Cavalier 2's departure in 1988. An interesting limited edition of just 6000 was the Commander, which had the Vauxhall griffin embroidered on the front seats in red, as well as the headrests — a nice touch and a car to look out for. Another limited edition was the special marque Club Cavalier, in saloon or hatch form offered in pure white. This was marketed alongside Club Novas and Astras, and featured colour-keyed bumpers, spoilers and wheel covers, low-profile tyres, tinted glass with a graduated shade band on the windscreen and bright seat facings, perhaps more at home on a deckchair.

Like the L type of 41 years earlier, the new Cavalier Mark 3 was driven around the Luton streets on announcement. Before this any TV viewer could have been involved in the launch. Special announcements were made during commercial breaks inviting the viewer to tune in at a certain time on a certain future date. Ford had executed this same trick with the new model Transit some years earlier, but this time the marketing men had really got their act together. When the time and date arrived, the special advertisement featured a "Car of the Future" seemingly straight from a late 1950s comic album. Of course the silver car was fictitious, although it certainly had a lot of people fooled. It had been built a few months earlier by a specially commissioned Midlands firm, and in fact it was just a rolling shell.

No estate version had been announced as this book closed for press, or indeed seems likely to be launched; the only derivatives are a four-door saloon and a five-door hatch. There are also four-wheel drive Cavalier versions, and, of course, the almost obligatory diesel engine derivatives.

This is the Mark 1 Cavalier at its most basic form, the 1300 L two-door. In place of chrome/rubber side strips, we see simple coachlines along the body flanks (except for the wheel arches). The doors, as on other models such as the Marina, Viva or Cortina, were longer on two-door versions, and the smaller rear side windows were of the non-opening variety. All Cavaliers (including the L) had rubber bumper strips; this idea became quite popular on contemporary vehicles until the decline in chrome, brought about by the trend towards polyurethane or plastic in the early 1980s.

Not too far from the Luton factory, this 1600 GL four-door saloon poses for the camera in Hertfordshire. Before the arrival of the Cavalier, Vauxhall had no competing model in the Marina/Cortina III "sales rep" market area. The Victors (then later VX 1800/2300s) were too large and far too thirsty; the Viva and Magnum saloons (and naturally the Chevette) were too small. The Cavalier fitted the niche nicely, making it a typical middle-sized family man's car, and it was not long before Vauxhall was selling many Cavaliers in this sector, and increased its percentage of the British market quite dramatically. Built at Antwerp, in Belgium, to start with, Cavaliers rolled off the Luton production line from 26 August 1977, creating many new jobs.

Model	Cavalier Mark 1
Dates of Production	November 1975 to August 1981
Body Types	2-door saloon; 2-door coupé, 3-door sportshatch; 4-door saloon
Engines Offered	1256 cc (57.7 bhp); 1584 cc (75 bhp); 1897 cc (90 bhp); 1979 cc (100 bhp)
Transmission	4-speed manual; or 3-speed automatic (except 1300)
Urban Fuel Consumption	31 mpg (1300); 28 mpg (1600); 27.5 mpg (1900 coupé)
Mpg at 56 mph	43.5 mpg (1300); 42.2 mpg (1600); 36.7 mpg (1600 auto); 37 mpg (1900 coupé); 39.8 mpg (2000); 36.2 mpg (2000 auto)
Top Speed	90 mph (1300); 98 mph (1600); 101.5 mph (1900); 106 mph (1900 coupé); over 110 mph (2000 sportshatch)
0-60 Mph	17.8 sec (1300); 14.3 sec (1600); 9.2 sec (2000)
Braking System	Servo-assisted dual circuit, front disc, rear drum
Wheels and Tyres	Wheels: 5 in rim pressed steel (L), 5 in rim styled sports (GL), $5\frac{1}{2}$ in rim styled sports (hatch & coupé); tyres: 165SR x 13 (saloon models) 185HR x 13 (sportshatch coupé)
Dimensions	Length: 14 ft 6 in (sportshatch 14 ft $2\frac{1}{2}$ in); width: 5 ft $5\frac{1}{10}$ in (sportshatch 5 ft); height: 4 ft $3\frac{7}{10}$ in (coupé 4 ft $2\frac{3}{10}$ in, sportshatch 4 ft 2 in)
Weight	Saloons: 1973 lb (1300L 2-door); 2017 lb (1300L 4-door) 2094 lb (1600L 2-door); 2183 lb (1600L 4-door) 2138 lb (1600GL 4-door); 2205 lb (2000GL 4-door) Coupés: 2227 lb (1900GL/GLS); 2205 lb (2000GLS)
Price at Launch	£1688
Made at	Luton (from 26 August 1977) & Belgium
Number Produced	UK sales of sportshatch/coupé: 16,735; total Mark 1: 248,440
Also available as	Opel Ascona/Manta

An interior study of a Cavalier 1300GL in left-hand-drive four-door export form unusual for a Cavalier as the nearly identical Opel Ascona (there were some differences in the front end styling and detail badging) normally took care of European sales. British versions never had the option of GL trim on this model with its 1256 cc Chevette/Viva power train, nor the headrests just visible here. The stubby Chevette-type gear lever and a control for the manual choke were the only items that distinguished the interior from the larger-engined 1.6-, 1.9- and later 2-litre versions. The marketing text beneath this official Vauxhall press photograph stated that 1256 cc and 1600 cc coupé versions were also to be introduced models that never were! **Above right:** *The sportshatch joined the Cavalier line-up in September 1978. At first it was on the production line with the coupé, but was soon to supersede it. Available as the 2000GLS (or with the optional 1600 cc power unit), the two-door fastback shared its wheelbase, mechanics and floorpan with the existing Cavaliers (and indeed the same pointed rear lamp clusters as the coupé). Challenging high performance vehicles such as the Lancia Beta and Reliant Scimitar, it became the first Cavalier with fold-down rear seats. Its fastback styling (and larger, more deeply raked windscreen) helped to push the 2-litre version of the vehicle to 107 mph, with 0–60 mph of 11 sec. The sportshatch, which carried side motifs at the bottom of its B pillars, was dearer than similarly engined and trimmed saloon models. The similar Opel Manta versions were continued until late 1988, giving basically an uninterrupted 13-year production run for this car.*

Available from the start of Cavalier production as a 1900GL, this particularly early coupé (registered in January 1976, making it one of the first 50 or so) reveals the high handling capabilities that can be achieved; the car is being driven by its owner, Lindon Lait of Ipswich, Suffolk, at considerable speed into this 90° bend. The coupé finally ceased production in 1979, making room for the newer sportshatch Cavalier. Another Vauxhall classic? A total of 16,535 coupés and sportshatches were built between 1975 and 1981. Perhaps in a couple of decades the model will have been completely forgotten and referred to as the ubiquitous Opel Manta — the German equivalent that ran from 1975 to 1988. Just for the record, there were three "official" Cavalier coupés from November 1975 to September 1976 the 1900GL; followed by the 1900GLS from September 1976 to March 1978; and finally the 2000 GLS until August 1979 — indeed just in time for a few V-registered examples in Britain. Both sportshatch and coupé Cavaliers can be readily recognized from the front by their distinctive GRP front spoilers.

The concept of a three-door hatchback had figured strongly in Vauxhall's forward thinking since the early 1970s; indeed the "Silver Bullet", based on the sportshatch theme (a new word in the world of motoring in the early 1970s), is featured elsewhere in this book. Here we see an official publicity photograph of the new Cavalier sportshatch of September 1978. In the background are two prototype vehicles on this theme. The rear vehicle, Concept 2, utilizes production doors, wings and bonnet. Even the integral looped bumper was bolted straight on to production sheet metal. However, with different B posts and altered rear design the contrast between this and the standard car is quite striking. Concept 1, the darker vehicle, was not based on any existing body or floor panels, or mechanical items. On this projected vehicle, rear seat passengers could enjoy more legroom by moving their seat back or forth. Note the by now famous Vauxhall identification remains here — the slanted nose cone.

Above left: The sporty SR hatch, also available in saloon form, displays its sloping rear end well here. Originally (for a few months at least) the SR, then the SRi, the model was equipped with the 1600 then 1800 injection engine until August 1987, when the 2000 cc fuel injected unit was adopted. The Cavalier became the typical sales reps car, regularly seen in the third lane of the motorway with the Sierras and Granadas. *Above right:* The car that turned the sales charts around for Vauxhall in the early 1980s. Six years after the introduction of the Mark 1 Cavalier saloon came an instantly successful Mark 2 — announced to the public at the 1981 London Motor Show, with an even greater number of trim/engine derivatives than before. Interestingly, this photo shows a rare two-door basic model that was very shortlived — although near-clone Opel Asconas continued in two-door form in Germany an unusual choice for the first of the line. Most evident (apart from the new, sleeker lines) is the use of plastic, now very much part of car designs today.

Cavalier Mk2 cutout

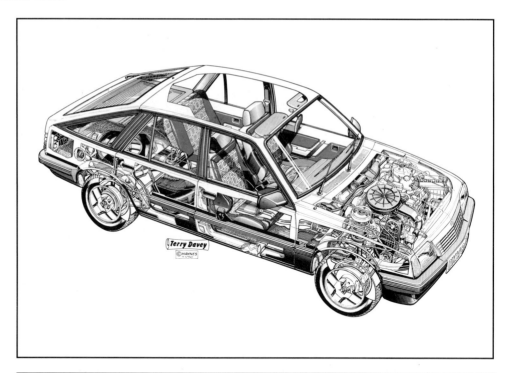

Model	Cavalier 2 (J car)
Dates of Production	August 1981 to October 1988
Body Types	2-door saloon; 4-door saloon; 5-door estate; 5-door sportshatch; 2-door Cabriolet
Engines Offered	1297 cc; 1598 cc; 1796 cc; 1998 cc
Transmission	5-speed manual; 3-speed automatic
Average Fuel Consumption	28-35 mpg
Mpg at 56 mph	40-55 mpg
Top Speed	87-119 mph
0-60 Mph	12 sec (1600); 9.3 sec (1800)
Braking System	Servo-assisted, front discs, rear drums
Wheels and Tyres	Wheels: SRi, $5\frac{1}{2}$J x 14; tyres: SRi, 195/60 HR14
Dimensions	Length: 14 ft, width: 5 ft $5\frac{4}{5}$ in; height: 4 ft 7 in
Weight	2068 lb (1300) – 2409 lb (CD)
Production Changes	The 2-door saloon deleted very quickly; estate versions from October 1983; October 1984: major face lift, new grille, interior, rear lamp treatment
Price at Launch	£4905 (1600L 4-door)
Made at	Luton (1st, 17 August 1981)
Number Produced	N/A
Also Available as	Opel Ascona; also similar to: Pontiac J2000; Holden Camira; Chevrolet Cavalier; Oldsmobile Firenza (2-door coupé), Cadillac Cimarron

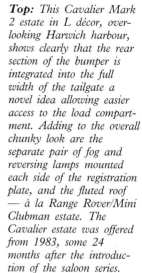

Top: *This Cavalier Mark 2 estate in L décor, overlooking Harwich harbour, shows clearly that the rear section of the bumper is integrated into the full width of the tailgate a novel idea allowing easier access to the load compartment. Adding to the overall chunky look are the separate pair of fog and reversing lamps mounted each side of the registration plate, and the fluted roof — à la Range Rover/Mini Clubman estate. The Cavalier estate was offered from 1983, some 24 months after the introduction of the saloon series.*

Middle: *Just as the Chevette was part of the worldwide T car project, Britain's Cavalier Mark 2 was part of the J car scheme. Besides its Vauxhall Cavalier and Opel Ascona manifestations, it appeared in similar form as the Chevrolet Cavalier and Pontiac J 2000 in the United States. All models had front-wheel drive, and British versions were 1300 (not the 1256 cc unit as before) and 1600 to start with, soon to be followed by an 1800. The estate took two more years to arrive.*

Bottom: *Modern dashboards on cheaper versions of popular cars have a habit of appearing comprehensive until closer inspection. Here we see this in a Cavalier L of 1984, showing us how plastic can be made to look good! Note the shorter, chunkier column-mounted stalkes. The famous Vauxhall griffin, in the centre of the steering wheel, has remained virtually unchanged since the beginning of the century.*

The super aerodynamic Cavalier Mark 3 of August 1988 was dubbed "the Car of the Future" and was heavily advertised on both the television and in the motoring press. This was the top model, the CD hatch, which had wood veneer once again, adding a touch of luxury to this £12,900 front-wheel-drive car.

Model	Cavalier 3
Dates of Production	October 1988 to current
Body Types	4-door saloon; 5-door hatch
Engines Offered	1389 cc; 1598 cc; 1700 cc diesel; 1796 cc; 1998 cc
Transmission	5-speed manual; 4-speed automatic; optional 4WD model
Average Fuel Consumption	24-42 mpg
Mpg at 56 mph	41-64 mpg
Top Speed	94 mph (1.7D) to 134 mph (2.0i 16 valve)
0-60 Mph	12.1 sec (1600); 8.6 sec (2000)
Braking System	Dual-circuit, servo-assisted, front disc, rear drums (rear disc on 2-litre and 4 x 4)
Wheels and Tyres	Wheels: $5\frac{1}{2}$J x 13 steel; $5\frac{1}{2}$2J x 14 alloy or 6J x 15 alloy; tyres: 165TR13 to 205/55 VR 15
Dimensions	Length: 14 ft 6 in (saloon), 14 ft 3 in (hatch); width: 5 ft 10 in (saloon & hatch); height: 4 ft 7 in (saloon & hatch)
Weight	2198 lb (1.4 saloon) to 2789 lb (2.0i 4 x 4)
Drag Co-efficient	Saloon/hatch: Cd 0.29; GSi saloon: Cd 0.30
Price at Launch	£7889 (1.4 4-door saloon)
Made at	Luton
Also Available as	Opel Vectra (some UK-built)

This is the Cavalier Mark 3 saloon in four-wheel-drive form, the cheapest car-derived four-wheel-drive vehicle on the market. Apart from some rather expensive late 1970s conversions on the Royale and Senator/Monza cars carried out by an outside company, no vehicle bearing the Vauxhall badge had ever been driven by four-wheel transmission before. This practical 4 x 4 model is powered by the familiar 2-litre transverse engine.

Model	Engine	From	To
CAVALIER 1			
Cavalier L 1600 2-door	1584	10/75	Autumn 81
Cavalier L 1600 4-door	1584	10/75	Autumn 81
Cavalier GL 1600 4-door	1584	10/75	Autumn 81
Cavalier GL 1900 4-door	1897	10/75	1978
Cavalier GL 1900 coupé	1897	10/75	9/76
Cavalier GLS 1900 coupé	1897	10/76	9/78
Cavalier L 1300 2-door	1256	8/77	Autumn 81
Cavalier L 1300 4-door	1256	8/77	Autumn 81
Cavalier Crayford Centaur convertible	1979	1978	1979
Cavalier GLS 2000 coupé	1979	9/78	9/79
Cavalier GLS 1600 Sportshatch	1584	9/78	Autumn 81

Cavalier GLS 2000 Sportshatch	1979	9/78	Autumn 81
Cavalier GL 2000 4-door	1979	1978	Autumn 81
Cavalier GL 1600 Sportshatch	1584	9/79	Autumn 81
Cavalier GLS 2000 4-door	1979	9/79	Autumn 81
Cavalier Silver Special 2-door	1584	12/79	–
Cavalier LS 1600 4-door	1584	7/80	Autumn 81
Cavalier LS 2000 4-door	1979	7/80	Autumn 81
Silver Aero Sportshatch design concept (one-off)	2400	1980	–
Cavalier Command Performance 4-door	1979	11/80	–

CAVALIER 2

Cavalier 1.3 saloon 2-door	1297	9/81	10/82
Cavalier 1.3 saloon 4-door	1297	9/81	9/88
Cavalier 1.3 L saloon 4-door	1297	9/81	9/88
Cavalier 1.3 L hatch 5-door	1297	9/81	9/88
Cavalier 1.3 GL saloon 4-door	1297	9/81	5/85
Cavalier 1.3 GL hatch 5-door	1297	9/81	5/85
Cavalier 1.6 saloon 4-door	1598	9/81	9/88
Cavalier 1.6 hatch 5-door	1598	9/81	9/88
Cavalier 1.6 L saloon 4-door	1598	9/81	9/88
Cavalier 1.6 L hatch 5-door	1598	9/81	9/88
Cavalier 1.6 GL saloon 4-door	1598	9/81	9/88
Cavalier 1.6 GL hatch 5-door	1598	9/81	9/88
Cavalier 1.6 GLS saloon 4-door	1598	9/81	8/86
Cavalier 1.6 GLS hatch 5-door	1598	9/81	8/86
Cavalier 1.6SR saloon 4-door	1598	9/81	10/82
Cavalier 1.6SR hatch 5-door	1598	9/81	10/82
Cavalier 1.6D L saloon 4-door	1598	5/82	9/88
Cavalier 1.6D L hatch 5-door	1598	5/82	9/88
Cavalier 1.8i SRi saloon 4-door	1796	10/82	8/87
Cavalier 1.8i SRi hatch 5-door	1796	10/82	8/87
Cavalier 1.8i CD saloon 4-door	1796	10/82	spring 87
Cavalier 1.8i CD hatch 5-door	1796	10/82	spring 87
Cavalier 1.6 estate 5-door	1598	9/83	9/88
Cavalier 1.6 L estate 5-door	1598	9/83	9/88
Cavalier 1.6 GL estate 5-door	1598	9/83	9/88
Cavalier 1.3 hatch 5-door	1297	9/83	9/88
Cavalier 1.6D L estate 5-door	1598	3/84	9/88
Cavalier 1.8i GLi saloon 4-door	1796	1/85	9/88
Cavalier 1.8i GLi hatch 5-door	1796	1/85	9/88
Cavalier 1.8i GLS saloon 4-door	1796	1/85	9/88
Cavalier 1.8i GLS hatch 5-door	1796	1/85	9/88
Cavalier Commander saloon Limited Edition (2400) 4-door	1598	5/85	–
Cavalier Commander hatch Limited Edition (3600) 5-door	1598	5/85	–
Cavalier 1.8i Convertible 2-door	1796	11/85	9/88
Cavalier Antibes saloon 4-door Limited Edition	1598	5/86	–
Cavalier Antibes hatch 5-door Limited Edition	1598	5/86	–

Cavalier 1.6D GL estate 5-door	1598	6/86	9/88
Cavalier 2.0i CD saloon 4-door	1998	8/86	9/88
Cavalier 2.0i CD hatch 5-door	1998	8/86	9/88
Cavalier 1.6D GL saloon 4-door	1598	10/86	9/88
Cavalier 1.6D GL hatch 5-door	1598	10/86	9/88
Cavalier 1.6 Club saloon 4-door	1598	3/87	–
Cavalier 1.6 Club hatch 5-door	1598	3/87	–
Cavalier 1.8i Li saloon 4-door	1796	4/87	9/88
Cavalier 1.8i Li hatch 5-door	1796	4/87	9/88
Cavalier 2.0i GLi saloon 4-door	1998	4/87	9/88
Cavalier 2.0i GLi hatch 5-door	1998	4/87	9/88
Cavalier 2.0i GLSi saloon 4-door	1998	4/87	9/88
Cavalier 2.0i GLSi hatch 5-door	1998	4/87	9/88
Cavalier 2.0i SRi 130 saloon 4-door	1998	4/87	9/88
Cavalier 2.0i SRi 130 hatch 5-door	1998	4/87	9/88
Cavalier 2.0i SRi saloon 4-door	1998	8/87	9/88
Cavalier 2.0i SRi hatch 5-door	1998	8/87	9/88
Cavalier 1.6 LX saloon 4-door	1598	10/87	9/88
Cavalier 1.6 LX hatch 5-door	1598	10/87	9/88
Cavalier 1.8i LXi saloon 4-door	1796	10/87	9/88
Cavalier 1.8i LXi hatch 5-door	1796	10/87	9/88

CAVALIER 3

Cavalier saloon 4-door	1396	9/88	current
Cavalier hatch 5-door	1396	9/88	current
Cavalier saloon 4-door	1598	9/88	current
Cavalier hatch 5-door	1598	9/88	current
Cavalier L saloon 4-door	1396	9/88	current
Cavalier L hatch 5-door	1396	9/88	current
Cavalier L saloon 4-door	1598	9/88	current
Cavalier L hatch 5-door	1598	9/88	current
Cavalier D L saloon 4-door	1699	9/88	current
Cavalier D L hatch 5-door	1699	9/88	current
Cavalier Li saloon 4-door	1998	9/88	current
Cavalier Li hatch 5-door	1998	9/88	current
Cavalier GL saloon 4-door	1598	9/88	current
Cavalier GL hatch 5-door	1598	9/88	current
Cavalier GLi saloon 4-door	1998	9/88	current
Cavalier Gli hatch 5 door	1998	9/88	current
Cavalier SRi saloon 4-door	1998	9/88	current
Cavalier SRi hatch 5-door	1998	9/88	current
Cavalier CDi saloon 4-door	1998	9/88	current
Cavalier CDi hatch 5-door	1998	9/88	current
Cavalier i 4WD saloon 4-door	1998	9/89	current
Cavalier 1.8 GL saloon 4-door	1796	9/89	current
Cavalier 1.8 GL hatch 5-door	1796	9/89	current
Cavalier 1.8 L saloon 4-door	1796	9/89	current
Cavalier 1.8 L hatch 5-door	1796	9/89	current
Cavalier 2.0 16V GSi 4-door	1998	9/89	current
Cavalier 2.0i 16V GSi (4x4) 4-door	1998	10/89	current

10

Astra and Belmont — Modern Economy

The Astra followed quickly in the footsteps of the new Opel Kadett, and unlike the Chevette had front-wheel-drive transmission. Astras were originally manufactured abroad, but soon production was transferred to Ellesmere Port, where the new model Astra is still being produced today. The choices were straightforward: there were three- and five-door hatch versions, three- and five-door booted versions (fixed rear window), and three- and five-door estates. Originally a super-economy no-frills-attached E version was included in the range; this was distinguished by its round headlamp treatment and bland interior. Top of the range was the Astra GTE, a designation borrowed from the Reliant Scimitar GTE of the 1960s and 1970s. It joined the fleet in 1983 and used the contemporary Cavalier's 1.8-litre engine.

The T85 Astra was built at Ellesmere Port from August 1984 and shown at the London Motor Show in October of the same year. A GTE became available immediately; unusually some of this model were in four-door form with a fully computerized dash, as used in the Senator.

Other models in the line-up included the normal SRi, Ls, GLs and Merits. The following year, the Astra was chosen Car of the Year by an international panel of judges. A limited edition Jubilee was marketed in October 1987, to celebrate 25 years of production at the Ellesmere Port plant. "Quick Silver" was a design exercise based on the two-door Astra GTE and was exhibited at the Birmingham Motor Show in October that year, as well as being displayed in the plant's showroom throughout the year. A 16-valve version of the GTE became available in early 1988, the 2-litre engine rendering it capable of 137 mph on the flat helped, no doubt, by its Cd figure of just 0.30. (Conventional Astras were 0.32 Cd.) Of course the GTE needed something equally as good to stop it, and so four-wheel disc brakes were fitted.

Unlike the Astra 2 of late 1984, the earliest Astra had no saloon version, and all models (except for those early booted saloons of the same shape) were all tailgated. To overcome this problem, just as Ford booted the Escort III (the Orion), so Vauxhall gave the Astra 2 a boot and named the new model the Belmont. The name Belmont had previously been used by General Motors in 1968, in the spartan Holden Belmont. Television advertisements were intended to appeal to the more astute potential customers, but the Belmont never sold that well. One unlikely model was the Belmont SRi, based on the Astra of course, but very few seem to have been produced.

Vauxhall amalgamated its Belmont and Astra ranges in January 1989, this coinciding with the introduction of the new 1.7-litre diesel Astra (previously a 1.6) and new CD models. The cars were now to become Astra Belmonts — that is except the original hatch versions. Part of this range included the Astra Belmont LXi estate (which Vauxhall called the "Sporting Estate"); this filled the gap left by the absence of a new Cavalier estate. Restyled instruments, a revised dash, and altered front and rear treatment further enhanced the model, which had by now lost its ugly chip-cut grille.

At the time of writing (November 1990), a replacement Astra is planned for late 1991 — seven years after the introduction of the Astra 2.

The Astra was yet another Opel look-alike, launched close on the heels of its opposite number, the Opel Kadett. Interestingly, the previous Kadett (similar to the Chevette) was phased out, and such was the demand for the older model that Vauxhall was soon exporting Chevettes to Germany! It took General Motors almost ten years to catch on to the European trend towards the "small car = front-wheel drive" formula. The first Astras were built by Adam Opel of Rüsselsheim, and the product range was complicated enough even to confuse the salesroom staff. There were three- and five-door saloons with a boot (for a while), three- and five-door hatch models (all very similar from a casual glance), and three- and five-door estates. Engines were offered in 1200 cc, 1300 cc, and 1600 cc petrol units — the 1600 cc diesel and special 1800 cc GTE type were soon to follow. The Kadett was also offered with a somewhat hard-worked 1 litre unit, although this continental engine never made it to Britain. Trim came in several alternatives Base, L and GL — soon followed by the sporty SR and GTE models. Note the alloy road wheels shown here on this early five-door GL model.

Model	Astra Mark 1
Dates of Production	February 1980 to Autumn 1984
Body Types	3-door hatch; 5-door hatch; van; 3-door estate; 5-door estate; 2-door saloon; 4-door saloon
Engines Offered	1196 cc; 1297 cc; 1598 cc; 1598 cc diesel; 1796 cc
Transmission	4-speed manual; 5-speed manual; 3-speed automatic
Average Fuel Consumption	27-35 mpg
Top Speed	95-115 mph
0-60 Mph	13.2 sec (1300)
	10.8 sec (1600)
	9.2 sec (GTE)
Braking System	Dual circuit, servo-assisted, front disc, rear drums
Wheels and Tyres	Wheels: 5 or $5\frac{1}{2}$J x 13; tyres: 155SR13
Dimensions	Length: 13 ft $1\frac{3}{10}$ in; width 5 ft $4\frac{3}{10}$ in; height 4 ft $6\frac{3}{10}$ in (saloon)
Weight	1895-2175 lb
Price at Launch	£3404
Made at	Ellesmere Port (from 16 November 1981)
Number Produced	105,649 to end of 1982
Also Available as	Opel Kadett

The customer may well have been unaware that his new Astra was built in Britain, at Ellesmere Port, Cheshire, where production had been transferred in November 1981. The Astra plugged the gap left when the last Viva had rolled off the production line nearly two years earlier. Of course, the Chevette had been built continuously at Ellesmere since 1975, but its sales soon tapered off when the Astra was announced. Astra Mark 1 production continued until late 1984.

First of the Astra GTEs is shown here (it was the Opel Kadett GSi in Germany), fitted with the 1.8-litre fuel-injected engine. Note the new Delco Freedom battery. The engine is still fitted to SRi Astras.

About a quarter of Astra sales were of the estate model a good-looking load carrier capable of taking 63 cu ft of luggage with the rear seat down. Available in either three- or five-door form, a car-derived van (no doubt replacing the phased-out ageing Viva HA van) joined the line-up in 1982, sharing many of the same components. The estate came 8 in longer than the saloon, the extra length all added behind the rear wheel line.

The flagship of the Astra range at first was the 1300S GL, which came in either two- or four-door form — hatch or saloon. By now it had become the norm to equip even small cars such as the Astra with rear wash wipes, adjustable mirrors, halogen lamps, colour-keyed velour cloth upholstery and carpeted load deck a far cry from the days of the little Viva HA.

The Astra E was available at the start of Astra production and, as its badge implies, was the most spartan of all Astras. The no-fuss instrument binnacle, thin carpeting, plastic seats and cheaper round headlamps were all features of this cost-cutting vehicle, normally offered to fleet buyers. It came in both two-door (shown here) and four-door form, with the fixed rear boot and 1200S engine.

Model	Astra Mark 2
Dates of Production	October 1984 to current
Body Types	3-door hatch; 5-door hatch; 3-door estate; 5-door estate; van; convertible; 4-door saloon (Belmont)
Engines Offered	1196 cc; 1297 cc; 1389 cc; 1598 cc; 1796 cc; 1998 cc; 1598 cc diesel; 1700 cc diesel
Transmission	4-speed manual; 5-speed manual; 3-speed automatic
Average Fuel Consumption	27-40 mpg
Mpg at 56 mph	45-70 mpg
Top Speed	95 mph (1.7 diesel) to 135 mph (GTE 16V)
0-60 Mph	12.1 sec (1300); 9.7 sec (1600); 7.6 sec (GTE 16V)
Braking System	Servo (uprated on GTE), front discs, rear drums; GTE disc all round
Wheels and Tyres	Wheels: SRi, Steel $5\frac{1}{2}$J x 14; tyres: SRi, 185/60 HR14
Dimensions	Length: 13 ft $1\frac{5}{2}$ in (hatch); 13 ft $10\frac{1}{2}$ in (estate); width: 5 ft $5\frac{1}{2}$ in (all models); height: 4 ft 7 in (hatch); 4 ft $8\frac{3}{10}$ in (estate)
Weight	2050 lb (SRi)
Drag Co-efficient	Cd 0.30
Price at Launch	£4494 (1.2 3-door hatch)
Made at	Ellesmere Port
Also Available as	Opel Kadett

The Belmont range complemented the Astra, in answer to Ford's booted Escort (the Orion) and the Rover 200 series. Basically, it was merely a re-engineered Astra Mark 2, with new rear treatment. In an uncommon guise, this is the injected 1800 SRi; this engine also powered the early T85 Astra GTE Mark 2.

Model	Belmont
Dates of Production	January 1986 to December 1988
Body Types	4-door saloon
Engines Offered	1297 cc; 1598 cc (82 bhp); 1598 cc diesel
Transmission	5-speed manual or optional automatic
Average Fuel Consumption	37 mpg (1598 cc)
Mpg at 56 mph	45-55 mpg
Top Speed	110 mph (1598 cc)
0-60 Mph	10.6 sec (1600)
Braking System	Dual-circuit, servo-assisted, front discs, rear drums
Wheels and Tyres	Wheels: 5J x 13; tyres: 155R 13 radial
Dimensions	Length: 13ft $10\frac{1}{10}$ in; width: 6 ft $5\frac{1}{2}$ in; height: 4 ft 7 in
Weight	2116 lb (1598 cc)
Production Changes	Renamed Astra Belmont from January 1989
Price at Launch	£9250 (1.8L)
Drag Co-efficient	Cd 0.32
Made at	Ellesmere Port

In order to bridge the gap left by the large Cavalier Mark 2 estate, the marketing department came up with the ingenious solution of upgrading the Astra L estate to become the LXi with an injected 1.8-litre power train from January 1989. It is worth mentioning here that although the Cavalier Mark 2 estate appears larger, the carrying capacity of the Astra is in fact slightly greater.

In January 1989 the Astra range was updated, and now included the Astra Belmont. Among new models were the luxurious Astra Belmont estate LXi, and the 1800 injection CD model illustrated. At last, the Astra had got away from the economy bracket, for the Astra CD featured wood veneer door trims, tinted glass and alloy wheels, as used on the new Cavalier CD. Note the new rear-end treatment; and the front valance has been dramatically altered with new grille, a round bonnet motif, high-pressure washer jets and integral foglamps, making this the most luxurious Astra ever.

Model	Engine	From	To
ASTRA 1			
Astra 1300S L hatch 5-door	1297	2/80	10/84
Astra 1300S GL hatch 5-door	1297	2/80	10/84
Astra 1300S L estate 5-door	1297	5/80	10/84
Astra 1200S E saloon 2-door	1196	10/80	12/81
Astra 1200S L saloon 2-door	1196	10/80	12/81
Astra 1200S E saloon 4-door	1196	10/80	12/81
Astra 1200S L saloon 4-door	1196	10/80	12/81
Astra 1300S L hatch 3-door	1297	10/80	10/84
Astra 1300S L estate 3-door	1297	10/80	10/84
Astra 1300S GL hatch 3-door	1297	10/80	10/84
Astra 1600S L hatch 5-door	1598	1/82	10/84
Astra 1600S GL hatch 5-door	1598	1/82	10/84
Astra 1200S E hatch 3-door	1196	2/82	10/84
Astra 1200S hatch 5-door	1196	2/82	10/84
Astra 1200S L hatch 3-door	1196	2/82	10/84
Astra 1200S L hatch 5-door	1196	2/82	10/84
Astra 1300S GL estate 5-door	1297	2/82	10/84
Astra 1600S L estate 5-door	1598	2/82	10/84
Astra 1300S E estate 3-door	1297	2/82	10/84
Astra 1300S L estate 3-door	1297	1982	10/84
Astra EXP hatch 3-door Limited Edition	1297	5/82	–
Astra EXP hatch 5-door Limited Edition	1297	5/82	–
Astra EXP hatch 3-door Limited Edition	1598	5/82	–
Astra EXPS hatch 5-door Limited Edition	1598	5/82	–
Astra 1600D hatch 3-door	1598	6/82	1983
Astra 1600D L estate 5-door	1598	6/82	10/84
Astra SR hatch 3-door	1598	9/82	10/84

Astra 1600S GL estate 5-door	1598	9/82	10/84
Astra 1600D L hatch 5-door	1598	4/83	10/84
Astra GTE hatch 3-door	1796	4/83	10/84
Astra Celebrity hatch 5-door Limited Edition	1297	3/84	–

ASTRA 2

Astra 1200S hatch 3-door	1196	10/84	8/86
Astra 1200S hatch 5-door	1196	10/84	8/86
Astra 1300S hatch 3-door	1297	10/84	8/86
Astra 1300S hatch 5-door	1297	10/84	8/86
Astra 1300S estate 3-door	1297	10/84	8/86
Astra 1300S L hatch 3-door	1297	10/84	10/89
Astra 1300S L hatch 5-door	1297	10/84	10/89
Astra 1300S L estate 3-door	1297	10/84	12/88
Astra 1300S L estate 5-door	1297	10/84	10/89
Astra 1300S GL hatch 5-door	1297	10/84	10/89
Astra 1600S L hatch 5-door	1598	10/84	current
Astra 1600S L estate 5-door	1598	10/84	12/88
Astra 1600S GL hatch 5-door	1598	10/84	current
Astra SR hatch 3-door	1598	10/84	8/86
Astra 1600D L hatch 5-door	1598	10/84	12/88
Astra 1600D L estate 5-door	1598	10/84	12/88
Astra GTE hatch 3-door	1796	10/84	3/87
Astra GTE hatch 5-door	1796	8/85	3/87
Astra 1600D GL hatch 5-door	1598	1986	1987
Astra 1600D hatch 5-door	1598	8/85	12/88
Astra Antibes 1.3 hatch 5-door Limited Edition	1297	5/86	–
Astra GTE hatch 3-door	1998	3/87	current
Astra SRi hatch 3-door	1796	8/86	current
Astra SRi hatch 5-door	1796	8/86	current
Astra 1200 Merit hatch 3-door	1196	8/86	current
Astra 1200 Merit hatch 5-door	1196	8/86	current
Astra 1300 Merit hatch 3-door	1297	8/86	10/89
Astra 1300 Merit hatch 5-door	1297	8/86	10/89
Astra 1300 Merit estate 3-door	1297	8/86	10/89
Astra 1300 Merit estate 5-door	1297	8/86	10/89
Astra 1600 D Merit hatch 3-door	1598	8/86	12/88
Astra 1600 D Merit hatch 5-door	1598	8/86	12/88
Astra 1600 D Merit estate 3-door	1598	8/86	12/88
Astra 1600 D Merit estate 5-door	1598	8/86	12/88
Astra convertible	1598	4/87	current
Astra GTE convertible	1998	4/87	current
Astra Shadow hatch 5-door Limited Edition	1297	10/87	–
Astra Jubilee hatch 5-door Limited Edition	1297	10/87	–
Astra Jubilee estate 5-door Limited Edition	1297	10/87	–
Astra GTE 16V hatch 3-door	1998	5/88	current

Astra Diamond hatch 5-door Limited Edition	1297	10/88	–
Astra Swing hatch 5-door Limited Edition	1297	10/88	–
Astra Swing estate 5-door Limited Edition	1297	10/88	–
Astra Swing hatch 5-door Limited Edition	1598	10/88	–
Astra Swing estate 5-door	1598	10/88	–
Astra Merit D hatch 3-door	1699	1/89	current
Astra L D hatch 5-door	1700	1/89	current
Astra Merit D estate 3-door	1700	1/89	current
Astra Belmont D	1699	1/89	current
Astra L D estate 5-door	1699	1/89	current
Astra Belmont LXi estate 5-door	1796	1/89	current
Astra CDi hatch 5-door	1796	1/89	current
Astra Belmont 1300 Merit	1297	1/89	10/89
Astra Belmont 1300 L	1297	1/89	10/89
Astra Belmont 1600 L	1598	1/89	current
Astra Belmont 1600 GL	1598	1/89	current
Astra Belmont SRi	1796	1/89	current
Astra Belmont CD	1796	1/89	current
Astra Tiffany 1.3 hatch 5-door Limited Edition	1297	6/89	–
Astra Tiffany 1.6 hatch 5-door Limited Edition	1598	6/89	–
Astra Belmont Tiffany 1.3 Limited Edition	1297	6/89	–
Astra Merit 1.6 auto hatch 3-door	1598	9/89	current
Astra Merit 1.6 auto hatch 5-door	1598	9/89	current
Astra Belmont Merit 1.6 auto saloon	1598	9/89	current
Astra Merit 1.4 hatch 3-door	1389	10/89	current
Astra Merit 1.4 hatch 5-door	1389	10/89	current
Astra Belmont Merit 1.4 saloon	1389	10/89	current
Astra Belmont 1.6 LX	1598	10/89	current
Astra 1.4 L hatch 3-door	1389	10/89	current
Astra 1.4 L hatch 5-door	1389	10/89	current
Astra 1.4 LX hatch 3-door	1389	10/89	current
Astra 1.4 LX hatch 5-door	1389	10/89	current
Astra 1.4 GL hatch 5-door	1389	10/89	current
Astra Starlight hatch 3-door Limited Edition	1196	6/90	–
Astra Starlight hatch 3-door Limited Edition	1389	6/90	–
Astra Starlight hatch 5-door Limited Edition	1389	6/90	–
Astra Starmist hatch 3-door Limited Edition	1389	6/90	–
Astra Starmist hatch 5-door Limited Edition	1389	6/90	–

Astra Starmist hatch 5-door Limited Edition	1589	6/90	
Astra 1.6 SX hatch 3-door	1598	10/90	current
Astra 1.8 SXi hatch 3-door	1796	10/90	current
Astra 1.6 SX hatch 5-door	1598	10/90	current
Astra 1.8 SXi hatch 5-door	1796	10/90	current
Astra 1.8 SXi estate 5-door	1796	10/90	current

BELMONT

Belmont 1.3 L	1297	10/85	12/88
Belmont 1.6 L	1598	10/85	12/88
Belmont 1.3 GL	1297	10/85	4/87
Belmont 1.6 GL	1598	10/85	12/88
Belmont 1.6 GLS	1598	10/85	summer 86
Belmont 1.8 GLSi	1796	10/85	12/88
Belmont 1.8 SRi	1796	10/86	12/88
Belmont 1.3 Club Limited Edition	1297	4/87	–
Belmont 1.3 Merit	1297	8/87	12/88
Belmont Jubilee Limited Edition	1297	10/87	–
Belmont Swing Limited Edition	1297	10/88	–
Belmont Diamond Limited Edition	1297	10/88	–

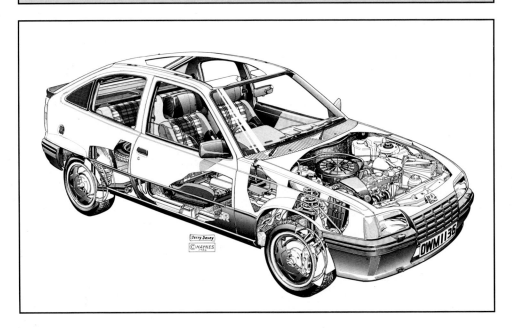

The New Carlton, Senator and Calibra — Modern Supercars

The disadvantage of writing a book such as this is that vehicles still in production are subject to change at any time. At the time of writing the current Carlton model has been around for over four years in both saloon and estate form. Launched in 1986, the bigger than ever Carlton 3 caused quite a stir. Its remarkably low Cd figure (0.28) is the result of a superbly engineered body, with flush-fitting side windows, mirrors and deeply raked windscreen, which allow impressive performance and low wind noise. The models were so well equipped that the press often wondered whatever else could be added to the specification. Needless to say, the Carlton received the Car of the Year award in 1987.

Five powerful engines drove the new models, all fuel-injected apart from the basic 1800 and, of course, the diesel variants. The top of the range was the 3.0 GSi, of which the *Guardian* newspaper reported: "It will outstrip many so-called sports cars while at the same time carrying five people and their luggage". A very potent, 24 valve, 3.0 GSi was added to the range in October 1989. This 3-litre six engine made its way into an estate car for a year, until replaced by the new 2.6 six late in 1990.

In the summer of 1987 the ageing Senator was replaced by a new version distinguished by its striking chip-cut grille. This, too, was based on the ACT (advanced chassis technology) principle. "Engineered for Unruffled Grace" was the sales slogan, and the top model CD competed against such rivals as the Ford Granada Scorpio and Rover 800 series. For 1989, the Senator 2.5i gained four-speed automatic transmission as standard, and both the 2.5i and 3.0i were equipped with ABS (anti-lock brakes). New spoked alloy wheels were adopted for the CDs, and even luxuries such as an on-board trip computer, cruise control, air conditioning and plush leather trim were all standard. For the 1991 model year, a 12 valve, 2.6-litre, fully green engine was introduced with a dual ram.

The London Motorfair of October 1989 was used to test public reaction to two very special new products, aimed at taking Vauxhall into the 1990s: the Lotus Carlton and the Calibra.

The Lotus Carlton had hit the motoring journal headlines in March 1989, when displayed in Opel form as the Lotus Omega. It featured a six-speed box that could boost the vehicle to 60 mph in 6 seconds and achieve a staggering 182 mph, with its twin turbocharged 3600cc six-cylinder 24-valve injection engine. The Motorfair "preview" sales literature stated: "Very few will be made. Very few will understand or appreciate its folly". It certainly attracted the crowds. Production versions differed slightly in design from this prototype.

Alongside was the Calibra. Claimed to be the most aerodynamic production car in the world, with Cd 0.26 on 8-valve models (the 16-valve's Cd figure is 0.28, the wider tyres no doubt contributing to the extra drag), the model was officially launched in June 1990. Pilot dealer showroom models came into the country via the Isle of Sheppey in Kent, where a keen eye could have seen dozens of them lined up at the docks that May.

A cabriolet Calibra would seem to be the perfect sports car — open air motoring combined with space-age technology. At the time of writing, rumours indicate that this will be forthcoming in 1992. However, it will not be built in Germany; Saab of Sweden are the likely candidates.

The Calibra, also called by the same name by Opel on the Continent, is the first all-green Vauxhall — no models are able to run on four-star fuel at all. Surely this must be the most exciting Vauxhall since the 30/98 of decades before?

The Mark 3 Carlton was Car of the Year 1987, and was powered by a choice of five engines 1.8, 1.8i, 2.0i, 2.3D, and 3.0i (i = fuel-injected), and came in both saloon and estate forms. The large estate car, was a keen competitor to the Volvo 740/760 series, and met a need by filling the gap left by the Ford Granada Mark 2 estate. The car pictured is a 2.0i CD saloon (featuring Vauxhall's ACT (advanced chassis technology), ABS and disc brakes all round.

Model	New Carlton
Dates of Production	October 1986 to current
Body Types	4-door saloon; 5-door estate
Engines Offered	1796 cc; 1998 cc; 2260 cc diesel; 2969 cc (177 bhp); 3600 cc (365 bhp)
Transmission	4-speed manual; 5-speed manual; 6-speed manual; 3-speed automatic; 4-speed automatic
Average Fuel Consumption	18-35 mpg
Mpg at 56 mph	36-52 mpg
Top Speed	From 96 mph (2.3D estate) to 182 mph (Lotus Carlton)
0-60 Mph	10.8 sec (1800); 10.4 sec (2000); 16.2 sec (2300D); 8.2 sec (3000)
Braking System	Dual circuit, servo-assisted, discs all round; ABS on top models
Wheels and Tyres	Wheels: forged alloy 15 in (3000GSi); tyres: 205/65 VR15 (3000GSi)
Dimensions	Length: 15 ft $4\frac{1}{2}$ in; width: 5 ft $9\frac{4}{5}$ in; height: 4 ft 9 in
Weight	3160 lb (3000GSi)
Production Changes	3000GSi joined range in Spring 1987; Lotus Carlton late 1990
Drag Coefficient	Cd 0.28 (saloon); Cd 0.32 (estate)
Price at Launch	£9250 (1.8L)
Made at	Rüsselsheim, West Germany
Also Available as	Opel Omega

Shown in pre-24-valve guise, this is the modern version of the 3-litre engine available in the new Senator and Carlton models. An awesome 177 bhp was available (204 bhp with 24 valves from the 1990 model year), which could hustle the Cd 0.28 Carlton with its new shape to speeds of 150 mph. This is the Green Age — the 24-valve is lead-free only.

Vauxhall had been accustomed to producing a straight six-cylinder almost since its foundation. Apart from a few lapses caused by odd marketing moves with Opel, six-cylinder motoring has constantly been at the forefront of Vauxhall production, and a feature of its prestigious models right up to this modern day Senator of May 1987. This is available in either 2.5-litre (140 bhp) or 3-litre (177 bhp) fuel-injected form, and 24 valve engined models boasting 204 bhp. This is the top CD Senator, available in 3-litre form only.

Model	Senator 2
Dates of Production	October 1987 to current
Body Types	4-door saloon only
Engines Offered	2490 cc (6-cylinder); 2594 cc (6-cylinder); 2969cc (6-cylinder) 2.6 Dual Ram 12-valve (150 bhp)
Transmission	5-speed manual; 4-speed automatic
Average Fuel Consumption	18-20 mpg
Mpg at 56 mph	35-40 mpg
Top Speed	2.5i: 124 mph (auto), 130 mph (manual); 3.0i: 134 mph (auto), 140 mph (manual); 3.0i 24 v: 146 mph (auto), 149 mph (manual)
0-60 Mph	9.3 sec (2500) 8.0 sec (3000)
Braking System	Dual circuit, servo-assisted, discs all round
Wheels and Tyres	Wheels: 6 in alloy; tyres: 205/65VR15
Dimensions	Length: 15 ft 10$\frac{7}{10}$ in; height 4 ft 9 ins; width: 5 ft 9$\frac{2}{5}$ in
Weight	3374 lb (3000)
Price at Launch	£14,830 (2.5i)
Made at	Rüsselsheim, West Germany
Also Available as	Opel Senator and Holden Commodore

The 24-valve 3-litre GSi Carlton, a strong competitor to Ford's RS Cosworth, also shown here. This genuine five-seater could top over 130 mph and yet still attain nearly 30 mpg when touring. Yours for £21,690 in 1989. Photograph Clive Hudson.

Vauxhall's entry into the 1990s the all-new Calibra, the most aerodynamic production coupé in the world. The car had made its début in England, at the 1989 London Motorfair. On launch, it was revealed that there would also be a four-wheel-drive model. Rumours indicate that a Lotus-developed Family II 16-valve 2-litre turbo engine has been shown at the Detroit Motor Show in a GM Pontiac Sunfire. This surely will be a candidate for a Lotus Calibra? Time will tell. Base model 8v shown here — with standard wheels.

Model	Calibra
Dates of Production	June 1990 to current
Body Types	2-door coupé
Engines Offered	1998 cc 4 cylinder (115 bhp 8 valve; 150 hp 16 valve)
Transmission	5-speed manual; 4-speed automatic
Average Fuel Consumption	25-30 mpg
Mpg at 56 mph	46-49 mpg (4x4: 42.8 mpg)
Top Speed	124 mph (8 valve auto) to 139 mph (16-valve manual)
0-60 Mph	8.1 sec (16 valve)
Braking System	Dual circuit, servo-assisted, discs all round, ABS
Wheels and Tyres	Wheels: $5\frac{1}{2}$J x 14 steel (8-valve); 6J x 15 alloy (16-valve); tyres: 195/60 VR (8-valve); 205/55 VR (16-valve)
Dimensions	Length: 14 ft $18\frac{9}{10}$ in; height 4 ft 4 in; width: 5ft $6\frac{1}{2}$ in
Weight	1194 lb (8 valve) to 1304 lb (4 x 4)
Drag Co-efficient	Cd 0.26 (8 valve); Cd 0.29 (16 valve)
Price at Launch	£14,700 (8 valve)
Made at	Rüsselsheim, West Germany

Road testers were hard pressed to find suitable testing sites for the 180mph Lotus Carlton, finally released on the market late in 1990. Autocar & Motor *commented "At 13 inches diameter, the disc brakes are so big, they'd raise a Mini's gearing if used as wheels". They needed to be large — at maximum speed, the Lotus covers 88 yards per second...*

Stronger then a Ferrari Testarossa or Lamborghini Countach, this 3615cc power unit offers 377bhp and as much torque at a leisurely 2000rpm as Jaguar's 5.3-litre V12 at its peak! Total Lotus Carlton torque is an impressive 419lb/ft.

Model	Engine	From	To
CARLTON 3			
Carlton 1.8 L saloon	1796	10/86	current
Carlton 1.8 L estate	1796	10/86	current
Carlton 1.8 Li saloon	1796	10/86	current
Carlton 1.8 Li estate	1796	10/86	current
Carlton 1.8 GL saloon	1796	10/86	current
Carlton 1.8 GL estate	1796	10/86	1988
Carlton 1.8 GLi saloon	1796	10/86	current
Carlton 1.8 GLi estate	1796	10/86	current
Carlton 1.8 CDi saloon	1796	10/86	1988
Carlton 1.8i CDi estate	1796	10/86	1987
Carlton 2.0i GL saloon	1998	10/86	current
Carlton 2.0i GL estate	1998	10/86	current
Carlton 2.0i CD saloon	1998	10/86	current
Carlton 2.0i CD estate	1998	10/86	current
Carlton 2.3 D L saloon	2260	10/86	current
Carlton 2.3 D L estate	2260	10/86	current
Carlton 3.0 GSi saloon	2969	3/87	10/89
Carlton 2.0i CDX saloon	1998	1988	current
Carlton 2.0i CDX estate	1998	11/88	current
Carlton Voyager estate Limited Edition	1998	5/89	–
Carlton 3.0i CDX estate	2969	9/89	10/90
Carlton 3.0 GSi 24V	2969	10/89	current
Lotus Carlton	3615	11/90	current
Carlton 2.6i CDX saloon	2594	10/90	current
Carlton 2.6i CDX estate	2594	10/90	current
SENATOR 2			
Senator 2.5i	2490	9/87	10/90
Senator 3.0i	2969	9/87	current
Senator 3.0i CD	2969	9/87	current
Senator 2.6i	2594	10/90	current
Senator 3.0i 24V	2969	10/90	current
CALIBRA COUPÉ			
Calibra 8V	1998	6/90	current
Calibra 16V	1998	6/90	current
Calibra 16V (4x4)	1998	11/90	current

12

Rare Sports Classics

This chapter is devoted to sporting derivatives of regular family cars described elsewhere in the book. These versions are distinctive enough to warrant being picked out for this separate treatment. The omission here is the VX 4/90, a sporting type that has been given its own chapter.

After the launch of the HB, the Jack Brabham Racing Organization was soon to strike a deal with the Vauxhall works, and marketed their Brabham Viva. As far as the public was concerned, this was a model in its own right; the truth of the matter was that it was a specified conversion carried out by local dealers. Existing Viva 90s, either new or secondhand, were used and when the conversion was completed, attractive side flash treatment was added to the bonnet, and extended along the body flanks and on to the doors. These side flashes are sadly no longer available. Worthy of mention is the HB Brabham Torana (no transfers — all metal badging) of Australia. This hotted-up Viva was marketed "to give the Holden small-car range a better image"; but unfortunately, information on this two-decade-old car is very scarce.

Despite the sporting machines of its early, "Prince Henry" days, Vauxhall seemed always to be slightly conservative in approach, producing very few cars — apart from obvious conversions such as the Brabham — to attract the young and sport-minded owner. That was the position until the introduction of the Viva GT, a hot-blooded 2-litre with enough charisma to separate it firmly from its saloon stablemates. There were two versions of the GT and tuning wizard Bill Blydenstein, who was so successful in racing the vehicle, offered extra modifications to enhance the performance still further.

Vauxhall could almost be accused of overdoing it. The earliest GT could be easily identified by a black bonnet, and chrome and silver wheels. Basically, the car looked too cheap, and so a "Phase 2" GT was introduced soon after, this time more conservative with Rostyle wheels and bonnet the same colour as the body. Both the GTs had a unique bonnet, with twin bonnet air scoops that actually served a purpose in cooling the engine compartment. This design was brought back to the Astra GTE Mark 2.

Although no evidence remains to suggest this, it is likely that the Brabham Viva was discontinued in favour of the GT, of which a total 4606 were sold (many abroad), until it too was discontinued with the introduction of the HC series. An active section of the Viva Owners' Club deals solely with the location of Viva GTs.

At first there was no sports model in the new HC line-up. However, in May 1971 the Firenza arrived, as styled by David Jones, Vauxhall's head of styling for many years. He had even been responsible for the styling of the little pre-war Ten coupé described in Chapter 1, and if you squint long enough it is possible to see a resemblance! Confusing was the fact that in the beginning the Firenza utilized the 1159 cc Viva engine. However, when the 1256 Viva came along later in the year this latter unit was fitted. And furthermore, just as the 1800 engine had superseded the 1600 ex-HB unit (optional in the Viva), the Firenza, too, made use of this unit; thus the 1600 had gone for ever. What is more, the Firenza came in the guise of a 2300 SL and 2300 Sport (the latter identified by its transfer strip badge on the right-hand side of the boot lid), with a full seven-dial instrument binnacle. In fact, each engine size (after the 1159 cc and 1600 cc versions had gone) had its own set of instruments.

The short-lived Firenza models, which sold in their respective two-year production runs, were superseded by the Viva Magnum (to give it its correct title, although it was never badged as such). The Viva Magnum still took care of

Giving a model the sporting GT badge was a brave move for Vauxhall. This occurred in 1968 with the introduction of the slant four 1975 cc 112 bhp Viva GT. A new breed of Vauxhall drivers was lured in by exciting, and tempting, speeds of over 100 mph in this small-bodied car. Unlike the more conservative-looking Mark 2 version, earliest GTs had matt-black bonnets (the paint extended to the tops of the wings, no doubt making resprays very difficult) and garish wheels complete with chrome wheel trims. The latter gave the regrettable impression that the driver had popped into his local Motorists' Goodies Centre and jazzed the car up! The bonnet moulding was separate, not shared with the standard HB car. Those scoops were actually part of the bonnet pressing rather than "stuck-on-afterward" units, as might be thought after a casual glance. This makes spare GT bonnets today as rare as the proverbial hen's teeth. A full seven-dial dash added to the sporty feel of what must now be only a few hundred surviving Viva GTs out of the 4606 built (many of which were exported).

the sporting end of the Viva market. However, this time it offered, like the Viva, two- and four-door saloons, a short-lived two-door coupé and a three-door fast-back estate, all with a reasonably high level of equipment. The Magnums, all identified by wider tyres and black grille with twin headlamps (the earliest standard Firenzas had a silver grille) finally ceased in 1978. To use up surplus stocks of the 1800 cc slant four engine after the demise of the FE series that summer, a Viva 1800 GLS was offered, in automatic form only.

The press was eager to announce the introduction of a new high-speed silver-only Firenza in October of 1973, although it would be quite a while before any deliveries took place. *Motor* magazine reported that at Millbrook they had recorded some phenomenal speeds (at least on the large clear speedo), and suggested that over 130 mph would have been possible in one direction with the wind behind! The manufacturer's figure for the 0–60 mph time of 7.5 seconds proved to be a little too enthusiastic in reality, although the five-speeder did have plenty of power available. The Firenza was plagued with production problems, and was probably quite simply born at the wrong time. The three-day week in force at the time together with component problems eventually closed the door to Firenza production, which lasted only a few months. Happily, the Droop Snoot Group, an active British club, has on its register many

of the 204 built, and HP Firenzas are often well represented at Vauxhall club meetings. As a rough price guide, these much rarer models fetch anything up to one and a half times the value of a RS 2000 Escort of similar age.

It was the idea of the fastback Magnum estate mentioned earlier that gave rise to some interesting models. A one-off fuel-injected Sportshatch, registered GNK 31N, was evolved. This was styled by Wayne Cherry of Vauxhall. It used no fewer than six headlamps behind two glass screens within the fibreglass nose cone. This car is now safely in the hands of Vauxhall enthusiasts Mario and Edmund Lindsay, although sadly it has lost its fuel-injection system.

Another HC sports-orientated fastback was the official production Sportshatch, although this was a car that never appeared in the motoring weeklies' new car price lists. Dealers were soon to sell the attractive models without the need of advertising, and in any case only 197 were produced. Again a 2300 Sportshatch made use of spare nose cones left over after the demise of the ill-fated HP Firenza. All were finished in deep maroon with red bumper inserts and rain guttering, and featured the Magnum 2300 interior. Once again, quite a few examples survive and are in the hands of enthusiasts in the Droop Snoot Group.

An original Firenza 1600 SL of 1971 undergoing speed trials at Millbrook, the company's newly opened proving ground, known as "punishment park". In the background is the two-mile banked circuit used for speeds of up to 130 mph (although not in this model!). The curious fifth wheel is used as a very accurate method of measuring the car's true speed, fitted speedometers normally reading a little fast. The gentleman at the back is Gerry Marshall of Dealer Team Vauxhall, who has no doubt been testing some engine modifications to this Blydenstein-powered Firenza, as the badge on the back shows.

Model	Firenza HC
Dates of Production	May 1971 to September 1973 (HPF October 1973 to October 1975)
Body Types	2-door coupé, 2-door coupé "droop snoot"
Engines Offered	1159 cc; 1256 cc (62.5 bhp); 1599 cc (80 bhp); 1759 cc, 1975 cc (80 bhp); 2279 cc (131 bhp)
Transmission	4-speed manual; 3-speed automatic; 5-speed on HP Firenza
Average Fuel Consumption Mpg at 56 mph	26 mpg (1975 cc); 34 mpg (1159 cc) 33 mpg (1975 cc)
Top Speed	80 mph (1159 cc); 100 mph (1975 cc); over 115 mph (HPF)
0-60 Mph	19.4 sec (1159 cc); 11.8 sec (1975 cc); 9.4 sec (HP Firenza)
Braking System	Servo-assisted, front discs, rear drums
Wheels and Tyres	Wheels: 5J x 13 (HPF: Alloy 6JK x 13); tyres: 165 – 70HR143 radial (HPF: 185/70 HR13)
Dimensions	Length: 13 ft 6 in; width: 5 ft 5 in; height: 4 ft 5 in
Weight	1882 lb (1159 cc); 2296 lb (HPF)
Production Changes	Engine range altered March 1972
Price at Launch	£973 (HPF £2625)
Made at	Luton (Sportshatch only at Ellesmere Port)
Number Produced	1971 (smaller engined): 13,312 1972-3 (larger engined): 5,140 HP Firenza: 204 only
Notes	An HP Firenza achieved a best one-way indicated speed of over 130 mph, in *Motor* 1973

Depending on which set of figures you read, production of the HP Firenza (HP = high performance) of 1973–5 was very low; apparently 203 were produced plus a single left-hand-drive example, and all in stunning Silver Starfire metallic. It was intended to be a success; it was hoped to produce over 1000 a year and indeed, there are reports that there was "capacity for between 20,000 and 50,000 to be made". The vehicle was plagued with problems; the fibreglass nose cone was difficult to graft into position and had to be hand finished; and just after the official launch in late 1973 came the three-day week in Britain in which HP Firenza components were given very low priority. Nevertheless, the vehicle still looks modern nearly two decades later, and at least half the Firenzas survive and fetch a good price on the second-hand classic car market.

A thick black leather covering to the steering wheel rim, full seven-dial instrumentation and passenger grab rail on the facia (and this was certainly needed), were eye-catching identifying cockpit features of the high performance Firenza "droop snoot" of October 1973. The light-grey seats were deeply upholstered for added comfort on long journeys, but lacked headrests.

Again, powered by the twin-carburettor version of the overhead camshaft slant four engine, the new Magnum coupé looked little different from its immediate predecessor, the Firenza 2300SL. This car was available alongside the more expensive HP Firenza, which easily out accelerated it. The Magnum coupé lasted until 1975, when merely deleted from the Magnum range, which in turn was sold through until 1978. Note the unusual adoption of chrome wheel rims on the Rostyle wheels.

Model	Magnum HC
Dates of Production	October 1973 to February 1978 (production suspended May to October 1976)
Body Types	2-door; 2-door coupé; 4-door; 3-door estate
Engines Offered	1759 cc (77/88 bhp); 2279 cc (108/110 bhp)
Transmission	4-speed manual; 3-speed automatic
Average Fuel Consumption	30 mpg (1800); 25 mpg (2300)
Mpg at 56 mph	33 mpg (1800); N/A (2300)
Top Speed	93 mph (1800); 103 mph (2300)
0-60 Mph	12.6 sec (1800); 10 sec (2300)
Braking System	Servo-assisted, front disc, rear drums
Wheels and Tyres	Wheels: Rostyle or styled steel 5J x 13 in; tyres: (1800) 155 x 135SR radial; (2300) 175/70 x 13 radial

Dimensions	Length: 13 ft 6 $\frac{9}{10}$ in; width: 5 ft 4 $\frac{7}{10}$ in; height: 4 ft 5 $\frac{1}{10}$ in
Weight	1800: (2-door) 2135 lb; 2175 lb (4-door); 2130 lb (coupé); 2250 lb (estate); 2300: 2155 lb (2-door); 2195 lb (4-door); 2150 lb (coupé); 2269 lb (estate)
Production Changes	No significant changes, although coupé shortlived; Autumn 1975: 1800 given 2300 seven-dial instrumentation
Price at Launch	£1644
Made at	Ellesmere Port
Number Produced	14,921 (saloons) 1692 (coupés) 3687 (estates) 197 (sportshatches)

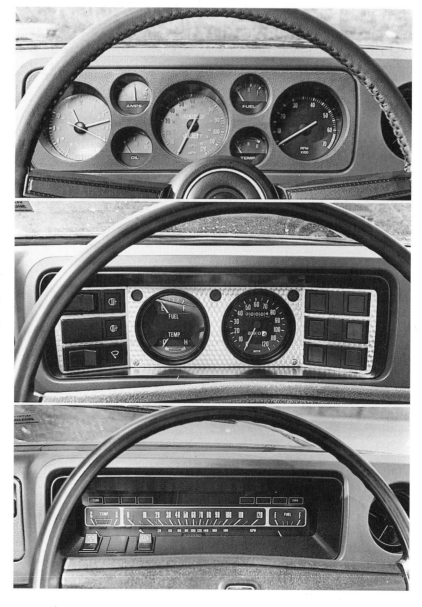

Firenzas came in three engine sizes by late 1972, and each model had its own set of instruments. The basic de luxe (1256 cc) more or less shared the Viva dash with the rather novel idea of headlamp and windscreen wiper rocker switches integrated, shown here at the bottom. In the centre is the twin-dial 1800SL dash, with four rather ugly accessory blanking plates (look carefully — the only added feature over and above the base model was the addition of a trip meter!). At the top, the still remarkably modern-looking Firenza Sport SL dash, with an engine shared by the rare 2.3-litre Vivas, and later featured in the even rarer HP Firenza, 2300 and last of the 1800 Magnums, and late 1970s 1300 GLS Vivas.

One of the 197 Vauxhall Sportshatches of 1976. This model never managed to make it into the official price lists, or indeed to have its own sales brochure — but it certainly was a car in its own right. Powered by the 2279 cc slant four, the Sportshatch came in one livery only deep maroon with red bumper inserts and side window surrounds. Wider tyres and seven-dial instrumentation added to the appeal, as did the HP Firenza's nose cone, which helped use up some of the surplus stock after the HPF project was abandoned. The venue here is Duxford airfield, where Mario Lindsay is shown about to wave a Droop Snoot Group member off in a timed club competition.

It's hard to beat the Chevette.

1st Mintex International Rally Feb 24/26

1st Finland Snow Rally Feb 17/19

At the beginning of the 1978 rallying season the Vauxhall Chevette 2300 driven by Pentti Airikkala has already scored two fine international victories.

At home and overseas the Chevette has earned a formidable reputation for strength and agility amongst the rallying fraternity.

But it's hard to beat a Chevette on the road too.

Chevette hatchbacks, saloons and estates offer unequalled versatility in their price range, and you can see them all at your local Vauxhall dealers now.

Test drive one soon. You'll realise that you could be onto a winner too.

SUBJECT TO OFFICIAL CONFIRMATION

Castrol

Dealer Team Vauxhall

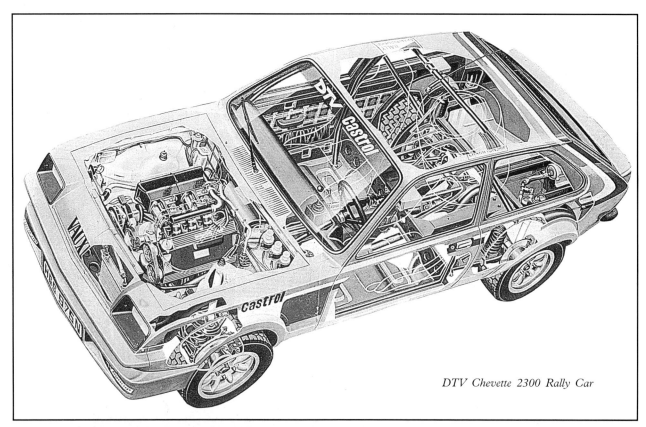

DTV Chevette 2300 Rally Car

The striking "Silver Aero" prototype based on the Mark 1 Cavalier Sportshatch. By the use of modern colours and a technically advanced interior, the styling department at Vauxhall managed to give this one-off a futuristic look. The vehicle survives and indeed passed into the hands of Vauxhall enthusiasts Mario and Edmund Lindsay, of High Wycombe, while this book was being compiled. It did not just look fast it truly was. It could certainly leave the Saab Turbo way behind, with 0–100 mph in 22.2 seconds, compared to the 30.2 seconds of the Swedish car.

The interior of the Cavalier Sportshatch certainly did not disappoint the occupants. Technically advanced seats, deep pile carpeting and plush door trims complemented the exterior design perfectly. When the author inspected the vehicle in late 1988, the condition was still as new, as seen here in this press office photograph.

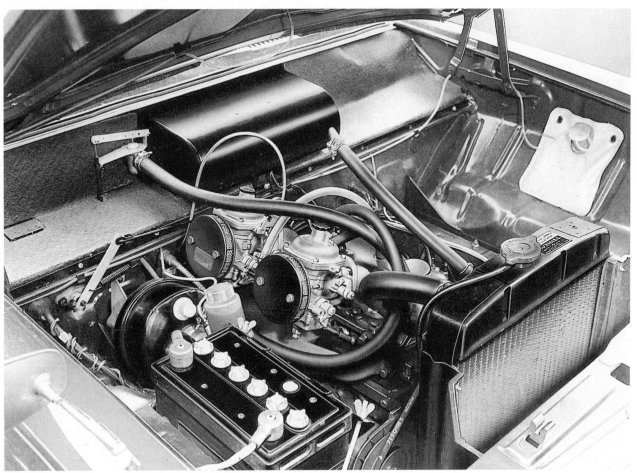

This heavily retouched photograph depicts the Viva engine after the Brabham treatment. Note the twin 150 CD carburettors, each fitted with a pancake air cleaner of its own. A new inlet manifold was also used and a big bore, straight-through exhaust was attached to the twin branch exhaust manifold. Remember those hanging windscreen water bags? Those were the days!

Model	Engine	From	To
VIVA HB GT			
Viva GT Mark 1	1975	3/68	7/69
Viva GT Mark 2	1975	8/69	9/70
FIRENZA			
Firenza De Luxe	1159	5/71	9/71
Firenza SL	1159	5/71	9/71
Firenza De Luxe 1600	1599	5/71	2/72
Firenza SL 1600	1599	5/71	2/72
Firenza SL 2000	1975	5/71	2/72
Firenza De Luxe	1256	9/71	9/72
Firenza SL	1256	9/71	9/72
Firenza De Luxe 1800	1759	3/72	9/72
Firenza SL 1800	1759	3/72	9/72
Firenza SL 2300	2279	3/72	9/72
Firenza Sport SL	2279	3/72	9/72
HP Firenza	2279	10/73	10/75
MAGNUM			
Magnum 1800 2-door	1759	9/73	2/78
Magnum 1800 4-door	1759	9/73	2/78
Magnum 1800 estate 3-door	1759	9/73	2/78
Magnum 1800 coupé	1759	9/73	10/75
Magnum 2300 2-door	2279	9/73	2/78
Magnum 2300 4-door	2279	9/73	2/78
Magnum 2300 estate 3-door	2279	9/73	2/78
Magnum 2300 coupé	2279	9/73	10/75
Sportshatch Limited Edition	2279	4/76	–

Note:
There was a break in production from May–October 1976.

2300 CHEVETTE			
Chevette HS	2279	1/78	1979
Chevette HSR	2279	1979	1981

13

Car-based Commercials

Although this chapter is concerned with the car-derived vans from Vauxhall, mention should be made of the CA and CF truck range, as many mechanical components from these vehicles were common to contemporary car production. Many of these vans will be remembered as motor caravans; a lot were converted and are in the hands of private owners who also, perhaps, ran Vauxhall saloons.

The CA was around from the early 1950s (even a "finned" American model existed in the late 1950s); and the CF was produced with the same basic shape from its introduction in 1969. The CA came in petrol-engined form only, with the choice of either sliding doors or the normal front-hinged variety. By the early 1960s the rather ugly grille had been changed in favour of an attractive chrome unit. The CF enjoyed similar success and it, too, was subject to a new front end, which by the early 1980s could be completely detached from the front of the vehicle for thorough servicing. Despite its arguably better looks the CF, originally powered by the slant four 1600 and 2000 units, then the FE's 1800 and 2300 engines, never had the success of the Ford Transit van. Like the earlier Transits, the earliest Opel diesel-engined versions were slow; the author remembers a 44 mph flat-out run from Romford, Essex, to Long Melford, Suffolk, in a 1976 example! However, the torque was splendid and despite the load, the CF would at least still pull well.

Apart from a few Continental conversions, Vauxhall did not produce any car-based commercial vehicles until August 1964, when the Viva HA van was introduced. This came in either 6 cwt (Type HAE) or 8 cwt (Type HAV) guise: Americans might prefer to think in terms of around 675 and 900 lb. The two models could be told apart, although virtually identical in shape. The 8 cwt had bright metal mouldings along the body sides (like the de luxe saloon), *chrome* bumpers and exterior rear view mirrors (these were painted on the 6 cwt), a metal finishing strip within the windscreen rubber, and various different interior features, such as an automatic interior light, full-width parcel shelves and rear floor mat.

An estate conversion was announced just a couple of months after the introduction of the van. Unusually, it took the name Bedford rather than Vauxhall, which was odd since it was marketed as an estate version of the HA saloon. This conversion was based on the 8 cwt van, and once again was carried out at Folkestone by Martin Walter, whose Motor Show sales motto was, "Don't poodle about, better buy Beagle". Essentially, the van emerged from the works with four seats, side windows, more trim and a cheap price tag of £624. A Mark 2 Beagle emerged in late 1965, with a padded facia and a decorative flash on each side. Because of its high wind resistance this estate car could barely reach 70 mph, and despite its attractive size the conversion was easily outsold by Mini 1000 Travellers and Ford Anglia estates.

The commercial HA continued in production through the HB Viva era, and in January 1973 a smart limited edition "Hi-line" version was made available in deep metallic blue with chrome wheel trims and a rear row of seats. Naturally, contemporary HAs had the Viva engine of the day, and so a total of three power units had been used by the time of the model's demise in the early 1980s. No diesel was ever produced. Such was the longevity of this popular little van, it even outlasted the Viva HC!

In 1976 the Chevette, having been established for well over a year, became available in van form, called the Chevanne, with the same body style as the estate. This was an odd move in marketing terms since the little HA van was still to be produced alongside the 13-year-younger Bedford Chevanne, which used the same engine. No doubt a contributory factor was HA's loyal corporate customers, who included British Rail, the Gas and Electricity Boards, and the GPO. The Chevanne also lasted into the early 1980s. It was finally axed with the introduction of the original Astra in 1982, which won the Van of the Year award in 1983.

The new T85 Astra 2 was announced at the end of 1984, and two van types were offered. The normal van body was kept for one version, but a clever

Motorized caravans are always well looked after and last a long time; this early 1960s Bedford CA Dormobile is no exception. Note the elevating roof section, two-tone coachwork, and chrome wheel hubs on this recently photographed, very tidy example. Another version was the CA Grosvenor conversion of 1953. The CA was launched in the early 1950s and lasted a decade and a half until replaced by the Bedford CF in 1969. As with the CF, some versions were equipped with sliding doors, like the one pictured here.

Astramax commercial was designed. This resembled the popular car-based Fiat vans and Matra Ranchos where the roof line was extended way above the cab roof, from immediately behind. This drastically improved the carrying capacity and produced a very popular all-rounder. By 1989 there was a choice of three engine types: a 1.3-, a 1.6- and a 1.7-litre diesel; the last-mentioned replaced the earlier 1.6 derv-powered unit. The later new frontal treatment of the 1989 Astras was also extended to the van range.

Summer 1990 brought the demise of the Bedford name; all commercials are now to be Vauxhalls. October 1990 saw the Vauxhall Albany appear on the new car price lists in the motoring press, essentially a van-type personnel carrier for the 1990s. Seven seats, stereo radio and a 2-litre engine, Vauxhall has paved the way for the big British manufacturers to compete with the Japanese.

The ubiquitous Bedford CF van, available in a variety of guises, superseded the CA in 1969. It remained the main rival, in Britain at least, to the Ford Transit van throughout its production run. Shown here is a 3.3-ton gvw CF chassis unit fitted with steel dropside body in the vehicle's earliest form. Note the use of a twin rear wheel axle on this model. Power normally came from current production car engines, albeit often in detuned form. Top of the range CFs had chromium-plated bumpers. Diesel versions were available, the earliest Opel-engined version being particularly slow 45 mph was a realistic top speed. Earliest surviving CFs include many well-looked-after motor caravan conversions. Series II CFs had a cleverly designed front the whole of the front grille/bumper/lamp assembly could be removed for ease of servicing.

The little Viva van arrived a year after the HA saloon in mid-1964 and gained many loyal corporate customers such as the Post Office, British Telecom, British Rail (shown here), and the various Gas and Electricity Boards. Available in either 6 or 8 cwt versions, they were powered by the contemporary Viva engines 1063 cc (HA car), 1159 cc (HB and early HC), and 1256 cc (the HC). No diesel-engined version was ever offered. From 1975 the HA van had competition from the same stable the Chevanne was born and used the same 1256 cc four-cylinder engine.

Bedford Beagle *Martin-Walter's estate car conversion of the Viva*

Price: £512 10s. plus £107 6s. 8d. tax = £619 16s. 8d.

Designed to be a busy Beagle

The Martin Walter Bedford Beagle is designed to do a variety of jobs extremely well. For family holidays or week-end chores, for load carrying or extended travelling, it offers speed, smoothness and comfort with remarkable capacity, 8 cwt. loading and all-round visibility unsurpassed by any other estate car in its price bracket.

1057 c.c. o.h.v. engine, all-synchro 4-speed gearbox, rack and pinion steering, hypoid rear axle . . . and, of course, typical Martin Walter quality apparent in the seating and interior trim. Choice of five factory finishes. £620.16.8 (including P. Tax).

Ask your local Vauxhall/Bedford dealer for further details, or post the coupon below.

'BEAGLE'

The Estate car with·the

pedigree

Model	HA	Chevanne	Astra 1	Astravan 2	Astramax 2 365 and 560
Dates of Prodn	August 1964-82	October 1978-83	1982 to Autumn 1984	1984 to current	1984-current
Body Types	Enclosed 6 cwt or 8 cwt	One only, as estate car	As 3-door estate car		As Astravan 2
Engines Offered	1256 cc; 1154 cc; 1057 cc	1256 cc	1297 cc; 1598 cc	1297 cc; 1598 cc; 1699 cc diesel	
Transmission	4-speed manual	4-speed manual	4-speed manual	Manual 4/5-speed; auto available on 1.3	Manual 4/5-speed; auto available on 1.3
Avr Fuel Cons. Mpg at 56 mph	28 mpg / 33 mpg	29 mpg / 39 mpg	25-30 mpg / N/A	See car 1.3: 51.4 mpg 1.6: 57.6 mpg 1.7D: 64.8 mpg	See car 1.3: 51.4 mpg 1.6: 57.6 mpg 1.7D: 64.8 mpg
Top Speed	70 mph	90 mph	95 mph	1.3M: 103 mph 1.3A: 99 mph 1.6M: 106 mph 1.7D: 96 mph	1.3M: 96 mph 1.3A: 93 mph 1.6M: 99 mph 1.7D: 87 mph
0-60 Mph	16.8 sec	14.5 sec	14.5 sec	As per car	As per car
Braking System	Early: drum; late: disc (f); drum (r)	Servo-assisted front disc, rear drum	Servo-assisted front disc, rear drum	Front disc, rear drum	Front disc, rear drum
Wheels & Tyres	4J; 5.50 x 12	Wheels: steel 5 in rims Tyres: 155SR13	Wheels: 5½J x 13 Tyres: 155SR13	Wheels 5½Jx13 155SR13 radials	Astramax 365: as Astravan. Astramax 560: 5J x 13 wheels 165SR13 reinforced radials
Dimensions	Length: 12 ft 7½ in Width: 4 ft 11½ in Height: 5 ft 0 in	Length: 13 ft 8in Width: 5 ft 2 in Height: 4 ft 3½ in	Length: 13 ft 10 in Width: 5 ft 4 7/10 in Height: 4 ft 7 in	Length: 13 ft 10½ in Width: 5 ft 5 7/10 in Height: 4 ft 10 7/10 in	Length: 13 ft 10½ in Width: 5 ft 5 7/10 in Height: 5 ft 5 7/10 in
Weight	1680 lb	1904 lb	2016 lb	1.3: 1929 lb 1.6: 1984 lb 1.7D: 2105 lb	1.3: 2017 lb 1.6: 2072 lb 1.7D: 2194 lb
Prodn Changes	Engine sizes changed in tandem with Viva car	As per car	As per car	As for saloon car	As for saloon car
Made at	Ellesmere Port	Ellesmere Port	Ellesmere Port	Ellesmere Port	Ellesmere Port

Bedford was happy to supply many car-derived vans to large corporate customers. These two Astra vans were part of the large fleet supplied to Hotpoint in February 1988.

What van can boast a Cd figure of just 0.34? The new Astramax (pictured here) is available in three power forms, including the new 1.7-litre diesel, as used in Cavaliers. It has a large carrying capacity, and one of the more interesting options is a pair of rear windscreen wipers, on the twin rear doors. Note the rather basic wheels, and old-style transfer decal mounted centrally on the bonnet.

	Engine	From	To
Viva HA 6 cwt	1057	8/64	9/66
Viva HA 8 cwt	1057	8/64	9/66
Bedford Beagle	1057	10/64	–
Viva HA 8 cwt SL	1057	5/65	9/66
Viva HA 8 cwt SL90	1057	5/65	9/66
Viva HA 6 cwt	1159	9/66	3/72
Viva HA 8 cwt	1159	9/66	3/72
Viva HA 6 cwt	1256	3/72	1982
Viva HA 8 cwt	1256	3/72	1982
Viva Hi-line HA	1256	1/73	–
Chevanne	1256	9/76	1982
Astravan Mark 1	★	1982	10/84
Astravan Mark 2	★	10/84	current
Astramax	★	10/84	current
Albany †	1994	10/90	current

Note:

L type vans (foreign-produced conversion): very rare indeed!

E type pick-ups: marketed in Australia 1951–8

V car van based on Rekord: Opel van in Europe, late 1970s/early 1980s, based on Rekord Caravan 3-door estate; sold in limited numbers in Britain.

Holden Gemini van: sold in Australia, with similar appearance and lifespan to "our" Chevanne

★ 1.3, 1.6 petrol and 1.6/1.7 diesels

† Actually van-based, but sold into passenger market

APPENDIX 1

MILESTONES IN VAUXHALL HISTORY

1857 Alexander Wilson, a marine engineer, found Vauxhall Ironworks, in Lambeth, London.

1894 Wilson leaves the company he founded.

1903 First Vauxhall cars produced: 10 sold in 1903.

1904 A 6 hp Vauxhall shines in the Glasgow–London Reliability Trial. Launch of 12/14 model.

1905 Vauxhall moves to Luton: about 50 cars produced; 7/9 hp models introduced.

  First 4-cylinder model: 18 hp.

1906 Bonnet flutes introduced on Vauxhall cars: lasted until 1982 and the demise of Mark 1 Carlton, Viceroy and Royale.

1907 Vauxhall Motors Limited formed, to concentrate on car production only.

1908 The 20 hp model introduced — one won the 2000 mile RAC Trials.

1909 B type 16 hp model announced. The 20 hp model gains speed and distance records at Brooklands.

1910 Vauxhall enters three 20 hp cars in Prince Henry of Prussia Trial. A Vauxhall is the first 20 hp car to exceed 100 mph at Brooklands Circuit.

1911 Vauxhall 16 hp car completes the Russian Reliability Trial. A modified 16 hp Vauxhall takes four world speed records. New 20 hp C type (Prince Henry).

1912 New 25 hp D model announced. Vauxhall works team enters French Coupé de l'Auto.

1913 The E type (soon known as the 30/98) launched. New 30/98 sets up new hillclimb record at Shelsley Walsh.

1914 A 30/98 comes second in Russian Grand Prix. GP Vauxhalls compete in Isle of Man TT race and French Grand Prix.

1914–18 Nearly 2000 25 hp D type staff cars built for the War Department.

1922 M type 14/40 14 hp announced.

1924 Vauxhall Motors withdraws from motor sport.

1925	Vauxhall becomes part of the General Motors Corporation of America. The 25/70 S type model introduced.
1927	R type 20/60 model in production.
1929	T type 20/60 replaces R chassis.
1930	Vauxhall Cadet introduced in 17 and 26 hp variants. T80 6-cylinder chassis in production.
1931	First Bedfords produced: trucks, buses and vans.
1933	A type launched (the 12 and 14 hp Light Six) and 26 hp 6-cylinder models introduced. First edition of *Vauxhall Motorist*.
1934	Independent suspension now fitted on Light Six.
1935	D type models introduced (12 and 14 hp). Production of Bedfords for Ministry of Supply began.
1936	GY and GL 25 hp models introduced.
1937	Vauxhall Ten introduced (H type).
1938	I- and J-types introduced (12 and 14 hp).
1939–45	At Luton 5460 Churchill tanks produced at Luton, and elsewhere from Luton-made parts, as well as over 250,000 Bedford trucks and other items for war effort.
1946	H, I and J models returned to production.
1948	L type Velox/Wyvern range launched.
1950	Bedford 7 ton models introduced. New $19\frac{1}{2}$ acre car production plant now operational at Luton.
1951	E type models introduced; Wyvern and Velox replace L types with these names.
1953	Golden Jubilee (50 years) of Vauxhall car manufacture. Over one million vehicles produced (including commercials).
1954	Beginning of £36,000,000 expansion programme. Luxury Cresta on E type body style.
1955	Bedford truck production moved to new Dunstable factory.
1957	First Victor (model F) produced. New top of the range Velox and Crestas introduced.
1958	New parts and accessories department opened at Dunstable. Victor estate announced; first factory-built estate car.
1959	Two millionth Vauxhall/Bedford vehicle built.
1960	Expansion at Ellesmere Port announced.
1961	Construction work started at Ellesmere Port. Victor and VX4/90 FBs introduced.
1962	Car production started at Ellesmere Port. Launch of 6-cylinder Cresta/Velox PB models. New engineering and design centre under construction at Luton.
1963	New small car announced: the 1-litre Viva HA.
1964	£36,000,000 expansion at Ellesmere Port announced. £2,250,00 engineering centre at Luton completed.

1964   First Viva HA models built at Ellesmere Port.
Victors redesigned — 101 FC launched.

1965   PC Cresta launched.
250,000th Viva produced.

1966   PC Viscount launched.
HB Viva models introduced; HA van production continued.
XVR experimental design vehicle exhibited.

1967   New service parts centre opened at Toddington, Dunstable.
FD Victor models introduced.
Diamond Jubilee year.

1968   Ventora announced.
Victor estates, and four-door Vivas offered.
Work begins on new 700 acre proving ground at Millbrook, Bedfordshire.
Vauxhall no longer available in Australia.

1969   Bedford CA van replaced by CF.

1970   HC Viva models introduced.
SRV research vehicle publicly shown.

1971   Dealer Team Vauxhall formed.
One millionth Viva model built.
Firenza launched.

1972   Transcontinental FE range introduced.

1973   Magnum models announced.
HP Firenza announced.

1975   Chevette hatchback launched.
Cavalier shown at London Motor Show.
Last edition of *Vauxhall Motorist*.

1976   FE models facelifted.
Chevette saloon and estate introduced.

1977   Luton-built Cavalier 1300 introduced.

1978   V cars — award-winning Royale and Carlton — introduced.
Cavalier Sportshatch announced.
Equus "concept" sports car shown publicly.

1980   Astra announced.
Viceroy announced.

1981   Cavalier Mark 2 announced.

1982   Carlton Mark 2 launched.
Vauxhall/Opel marketing merged.
HA van production ceased.

1983   Nova launched.

1984   Astra Mark 2 launched.

1985   Astra 2 awarded Car of the Year.

1986   Carlton Mark 3 launched.

1987   New Senator launched.

1988   "Car of the Future": Cavalier Mark 3 introduced.
First factory four-wheel-drive announced: the Cavalier.

1989   Vauxhall Calibra exhibited at Motorfair, London. The world's most aerodynamic production car — Cd 0.26.
Family 2 engine voted *Autocar & Motor* Engine of the 80s.

1990   All commercials badged as Vauxhalls from Summer 1990.
Corporate badge changed.
Calibra launched.
2,000,000th vehicle (Astra) completed at Ellesmere Port (August 1990).
Lotus Carlton introduced (November 1990).

APPENDIX 2

Total Production figures, 1903–82

Year	Vauxhall	Bedford	Total	Year	Vauxhall	Bedford	Total
1903	43		43	1944	–	34 124	34 124
1904	76		76	1945	–	38 773	38 773
1905	1*		1*	1946	19 713	33 809	53 522
1906	20		20				
1907	69		69	1947	30 376	31 077	61 453
1908	94		94	1948	38 062	35 522	73 584
1909	197		197	1949	44 999	38 144	83 143
1910	246		246	1950	47 692	40 783	88 475
1911	269		269	1951	35 219	43 382	78 601
1912	306		306	1952	35 127	42 969	78 096
1913	411		411	1953	61 260	48 445	109 705
1914	529		529	1954	72 129	57 556	129 685
1915	417		417	1955	75 634	67 933	143 567
1916	581		581	1956	64 453	63 226	127 679
1917	495		495	1957	91 444	58 783	150 227
1918	480		480	1958	119 177	55 439	174 616
1919	576		576	1959	157 365	88 720	246 085
1920	691		691	1960	145 742	106 284	252 026
1921	482		482	1961	85 370	94 595	179 965
1922	659		659	1962	144 144	76 661	220 805
1923	1 444		1 444	1963	164 987	84 798	249 785
1924	1 444		1 444	1964	247 782	106 672	354 454
1925	1 398		1 398	1965	227 344	113 825	341 169
1926	1 527		1 527	1966	172 177	101 898	274 075
1927	751		751	1967	196 882	89 296	286 178
1928	2 560		2 560	1968	247 034	97 925	344 959
1929	1 668		1 668	1969	169 456	101 821	271 277
1930	1 277	7 120†	8 397				
1931	3 492	11 487	14 979	1970	178 089	101 660	279 749
1932	2 136	10 529	12 665	1971	199 092	126 394	325 486
1933	9 949	15 173	25 122	1972	183 957	91 053	275 010
1934	20 227	17 823	38 050	1973	139 812	107 257	247 069
1935	22 118	23 741	45 859	1974	136 903	112 151	249 054
1936	17 640	26 210	43 850	1975	103 310	91 311	194 621
1937	30 616	31 783	62 399	1976	142 591	86 390	228 981
1938	32 224	27 474	59 698	1977	143 938	91 747	235 685
1939	34 367	18 185	52 552	1978	144 579	117 443	262 022
				1979	142 582	87 650	230 232
1940	18 543	54 696	73 239				
1941	–	39 873	39 873	1980	111 980	95 283	207 263
1942	–	46 761	46 761	1981	117 266	50 027	167 293
1943	–	48 648	48 648	1982††	187 078	53 047	240 125

* Move from London to Luton; London build records lost.

† 12 cwt and 30 cwt Chevrolets assembled; first Bedford trucks 1931.

††Based on actual figures to October and forecast figures to year's end. From 1976 totals include Vauxhall cars produced in other General Motors European plants.

APPENDIX 3

Motor Sport Achievements

1969
Gerry Marshall (Viva GT), 2nd overall, RedX Saloon Car Championship

1970
Chris Coburn (Viva GT), Team Award, Circuit of Ireland
Bo Brasta (Viva GT), 1st, Swedish Ice Racing Championship
Gerry Marshall (Viva GT), 4th overall (Group 2), Spa
Gerry Marshall (Viva GT), 1st (over 1300 cc), Orsam Saloon Car
Championship

1971
Reine Johansson (Viva GT), 1st, Swedish Ice Racing Championship
Gerry Marshall (Viva GT), 1st, Orsam Saloon Car Championship
Bill Dryden (Viva GT), 1st, Scottish Saloon Car Championship
Des Donnelly (Viva), 1st, Irish Saloon Car Championship
Jim Thompson (Viva GT), 1st, BARC Hillclimb Championship

1972
Chris Coburn (Viva GT), 1st overall (Group 1), Manx Rally
Chris Coburn (Firenza), 1st overall (Group 1), Dukeries Rally
Will Sparrow (Firenza), 2nd overall, Mintex Dales Rally
Gerry Marshall (Firenza), 1st, Forward Trust Saloon Car
Championship
Bill Dryden (Firenza), 1st, Scottish Saloon Car Championship
Jim Thompson (Firenza), 1st, BARC Hillclimb Championship

1973
Gerry Marshall (Firenza), 1st, Forward Trust Saloon Car
Championship
Bill Dryden (Firenza), 1st, Scottish Saloon Car Championship

1974
Pentti Airikkala (Magnum), 1st overall (Group 1), Thousand Lakes Rally
Will Sparrow (Firenza), 1st (Group 1), Rally Championship
Will Sparrow (Magnum), 1st overall (Group 1), RAC Rally
Gerry Marshall (Firenza & Ventora), 2nd overall, Simoniz Saloon Car Championship
Bill Dryden (Firenza), 2nd overall, Scottish Saloon Car Championship
Jenny Birrell (Firenza), class winner, Ziebart Saloon Car Championship

Derrick Brunt (Firenza), 2nd overall, Triplex Saloon Car Championship
Andrew Highton (VX 4/90), 1st, Repco Caravan Championship

1975
Gerry Marshall (Firenza V8), 1st Tricentrol Super Saloon Car Championship
Bill Dryden (Firenza), class winner, Scottish Saloon Car Championship
Dave Millington (Firenza), class winner, Forward Trust Saloon Car Championship
Plumb Tyndall (Magnum), 1st (Group 1), Bosch Plug Championship
Jenny Birrell (Magnum), 1st, Radio Four Saloon Car Championship

1976
Jimmy McRae (Magnum), 1st overall, Snowman Rally
Jimmy McRae (Magnum), 1st overall, Ulster Rally
Gerry Marshall (Firenza V8), 1st, Tricentrol Super Saloon Championship
Gerry Marshall (Magnum), class winner, Keith Prowse Touring Car Championship
Gerry Marshall (Magnum), class winner, Radio One Saloon Car Championship

1977
Pentti Airikkala (Chevette), 1st overall, Manx Rally
Pentti Airikkala (Chevette), 1st overall, Castrol 77 Rally
Pentti Airikkala (Chevette), 1st overall, Welsh Rally
Gerry Marshall (Magnum), class winner, Tricentrol Touring Car Championship
Gerry Marshall/Peter Brock (Magnum), 2nd overall, Spa 24-Hour Race
(Gerry Marshall: over 150 outright wins in Vauxhalls, 1966–77)

1978
Pentti Airikkala (Chevette), 1st overall
Hankiralli Finland
Pentti Airikkala (Chevette), 1st overall,
Snow Rally
Pentti Airikkala (Chevette), 1st overall,
Mintex Rally

1979
Pentti Airikkala (Chevette), 1st overall,
Circuit of Ireland
Pentti Airikkala (Chevette), 1st overall,
Scottish Rally
Pentti Airikkala (Chevette), 2nd overall,
Manx Rally
Jimmy McRae (Chevette), 1st overall,
Lindisfarne Rally
Pentti Airikkala (Chevette), 1st overall,
Ulster Rally
Jimmy McRae (Chevette), 2nd overall,
Ulster Rally
Pentti Airikkala (Chevette), 1st, Sedan
Products Rally Championship

1980
Jimmy McRae (HSR), 1st, Galway Rally
Jimmy McRae (HSR), 1st, Circuit of Ireland
Jimmy McRae (HSR), 1st, Donegal Rally
Jimmy McRae (HSR), 1st, Irish Tarmacs Championship

1981
Tony Davies (Firenza), Chevette Cup
Tony Pond (HSR), 1st, West Cork Rally
Tony Pond (HSR), 1st TV Rallysprint
Tony Pond (HSR), 1st, Scottish Rally
Tony Pond (HSR), 1st, Manx Rally
Tony Pond (HSR), 1st, Manufacturers' Championship

1982
Russell Brookes (HSR), 2nd, Mintex Rally

Russell Brookes (HSR), 4th, Scottish Rally
Terry Kaby (HSR), 6th, Scottish Rally
Russell Brookes (HSR), 3rd, Hunsbrook Rally
Russell Brookes (HSR), 2nd, Manx Rally
Terry Kaby (HSR), 2nd, Antibes Rally
Russell Brookes (HSR), 6th, RAC Rally
Tony Lanfranchi (Opel), Class Winner, Monza 24-Hour Race
(GM Dealersport formed January 1982, after DOT & DTV disbanded)

1983
Russell Brookes (HSR), 1st, Circuit of Ireland
Russell Brookes (HSR), 2nd, Welsh Rally
Russell Brookes (HSR), 3rd, Scottish Rally
Russell Brookes (HSR), 3rd, Manx Rally
Terry Kaby (HSR), 4th, Manx Rally
Russell Brookes (HSR), 5th, RAC Rally
Russell Brookes (HSR), 1st, (Group B), Open Series

1984
Jimmy McRae (Manta 400), Class Winner, British Open Rally Championships
Harry Hockly (Nova), 1st (to 1300 cc), British Open Rally Championships

1985
Jimmy McRae (Manta 400), 6th overall, British Open Rally Championships
Harry Hockly (Nova), 1st (to 1300 cc), British Open Rally Championships

1986
Pentti Airikkala (Astra GTE), 1st (Group A), British Open Rally Championships
Harry Hockly (Nova), 1st (to 1300 cc), British Open Rally Championships
Vauxhall overall winner, Manufacturers' Championship

1987
Pentti Airikkala (Manta 400), runner-up, Shell RAC British Open Rally
Championships
Brian Wiggins (Astra GTE), 1st (Group N), Shell RAC British Open Rally Championships
David Metcalfe (Astra GTE), 1st (Group A, Touring Car Class)
Warren Hunt (Nova), 1st (Small Touring Cars)

1988
Malcolm Wilson (Astra GTE), Class Winner (Group A), Shell RAC British Open Rally Championships
Brian Wiggins (Astra GTE), Class Winner, Shell RAC British Open Rally Championships
Colin McRae (Nova Sport), Class Winner (Class A), Shell RAC British Open Rally Championships
Mike Williams (Nova Sport), Class Winner (Group N), Shell RAC British Open Rally Championship
Mats Jonsson (Astra GTE), 1st (2-litre class) Lombard RAC Rally
Brian Wiggins (Astra GTE), 1st (Showroom Class), Lombard RAC Rally

1989
John Cleland (Astra GTE), British Touring Car Champion
Louise Aitken-Walker (Astra GTE), Class Winner, British Rally Championship

APPENDIX 4

Vauxhall Car Clubs
in Britain

Looking through any magazine on classic cars will reveal an apparent shortage of clubs in this country for Vauxhall enthusiasts and owners. For example, compared to the nine up-and-running clubs described here (plus three for combined Opel/Vauxhall), there are no fewer than 27 separate clubs listed for various Ford models, and 15 for Triumph. All Vauxhall models are, however, covered, for any particular type without its own specialist club, can be catered for by the OPEL–VAUXHALL Drivers' Club. As with many old clubs of this kind, the years have seen amalgamations, brought about by the increasing scarcity of a particular model. For example, the F Victor Owners' Club, formed in 1981, was extended to the FBs and became the F Victor Owners' Club & Register; and in 1987 the Vauxhall PA, E & PB Owners' Club took on board enthusiasts and owners of PC Viscounts and Crestas.

Each year, most of the clubs attend a meeting at Billing Aquadrome, Northamptonshire, which is certainly well worth a visit. Here then, is a complete list as at the end of 1990.

OPEL–VAUXHALL DRIVERS' CLUB

Formed in the mid-1980s, it caters for owners and enthusiasts of all Vauxhall and Opel passenger cars. Its newsletter includes information on Vauxhall motor sport activities.

Contact: The Old Mill
Bornow Hall
Dereham
Norfolk
Tel: 0362 694459

OPEL MONZA, OPEL SENATOR, VAUXHALL ROYALE REGISTER

This is a new division of the Opel Vauxhall Driver's Club and also welcomes owners of the 6-cylinder Opel Commodore and Vauxhall Viceroy models. See Opel Vauxhall Drivers' Club for contact details.

OPEL MANTA CLUB

Devoted to all Mark 1 Cavalier Sportshatch/Coupé models, as well as all versions of the Opel Manta from 1970 to 1989.

Contact: 8 Woodpecker Close
Twyford
Berkshire
RG10 0BB

OPEL MANTA OWNERS CLUB

A new club for all versions of the Opel Manta.

Contact: 14 Rock Stowes Way
Westbury-on-Trym
Bristol
BS10 6JE
Tel: 0634 379065

DROOP SNOOT GROUP (DSG)

Certainly one of the more thriving Vauxhall clubs, strictly for the owners of all 400 or so "Droop snoot" HCs, the Firenzas and Magnum Sportshatches, as well as the 400 homologation special 2300 HS Chevettes. Now a decade old, and represented at many events across the country.

Contact: 28 Second Avenue
Ravenswing Park
Aldermaston
Berkshire
RG7 4PX
Tel: 0734 815238

VAUXHALL OWNERS' CLUB

Catering for all pre-1957 vehicles (i.e. E types backwards), the Vauxhall Owners' Club is one of the more mature clubs, formed in 1976 for the preservation and use of all such models.

Contact: 2 Plaxton Court
St Leonard's Road
Ayr
KA7 2PP

VAUXHALL PA PB PC E SERIES OWNERS' CLUB

Perhaps more aptly called the VX Six Pot Club (except for the early Wyverns, of course), this club is concerned with the more expensive end of the Vauxhall product range from the early 1950s to 1972. This active group produces an excellent newsletter with more than enough members' advertisements for those obsolete parts, catering for over 500 members worldwide.

Contact: Steve Chapman
338 Eastcote Lane
South Harrow
Middlesex
HA2 8RY

VAUXHALL VX 4/90 DRIVERS' CLUB

A club for the owners of the faster and more attractive FD and FE models, spanning the period from the late 1960s to the now rare Phase 2 FE VX 490 of 1977–8. About 250 members — and growing.

Contact: Mike Nash
43 Stoudwater Park
St Georges Avenue
Weybridge
Surrey
KT13 0DT

VICTOR 101 CLUB

For the first "space-curve" Victor and VX 4/90, and all CA Bedford vans, and also for owners and enthusiasts of other Victor models. Owners of PC Crestas and Viscounts and other Vauxhalls are welcome to join.

Contact: Mrs L. Pearce
12 Cliff Crescent
Ellerdine
Telford
Shropshire

THE F VICTOR OWNERS' CLUB & REGISTER

With an international membership for followers of all F types and FB Victors and early VX 4/90 models.

Contact: Old Station
Eastville
Boston
Lincolnshire
PE22 8LS

VAUXHALL VIVA OWNERS' CLUB

An international club with nearly 400 members catering for all model HA, HB, and HC Vivas, including Firenzas, Magnums and Canadian-badged Epics. Formed in 1982, the Viva Owners' Club produces a quarterly newsletter, and pays particular attention to the location of HB Viva GT models — dead or alive!

Contact: Adrian Miller
The Thatches
Snetterton
Norwich
NR16 2LD
Tel: 095 382 8818

CA BEDFORD OWNERS' CLUB

For owners and enthusiasts of the few CAs left in existence — mainly motor caravans no doubt.

Contact: G.W. Seller
7 Grasmere Road
Benfleet
Essex
SS7 3HF

THE RADFORD REGISTER

All surviving Harold Radford luxury converted cars (not just Vauxhall) such as the extremely rare Radford Cresta, are the concern of this club.

Contact: Chris Gow
108 Potters Lane
Burgess Hill
West Sussex
Tel: 0444 648439

OPEN CAVALIERS

The rare Crayford Mark 1 Centaur Cavalier Coupé conversion, and the 1986–88 Mark 2 conversions, are the concern of this newly-formed club.

Contact: Ron Goddard
47 Brooklands Close
Luton
Bedfordshire
LU4 9EH
Tel: 0582 573269

Opel Vauxhall Drivers Club for contact details.

ROYALE, MONZA OWNERS' CLUB

Formed in June 1990 this club caters for the future classic Opel Monza and Vauxhall Royale Coupé models.

Contact: Trevor Godden
2 Caxton Court
Roman Road
Luton
Bedfordshire
LU3 2QS
Tel: 0582 597347